CHURCHILL

PROFILES IN POWER

General Editor: Keith Robbins

. . . . . .

CHURCHILL

Keith Robbins

LONGMAN
London and New York

Longman Group UK Limited
Longman House, Burnt Mill,
Harlow, Essex CM20 2JE, England
and Associated Companies throughout the world.

Published in the United States of America
by Longman Publishing, New York

First published 1992

ISBN 0 582 031370 CSD
ISBN 0 582 031362 PPR

British Library Cataloguing-in-Publication Data

A catalogue record for this book is
available from the British Library

Library of Congress Cataloging in Publication Data
Robbins, Keith
Churchill/Keith Robbins.
p.   cm. – (Profiles in power)
Includes bibliographical references and index.
ISBN 0–582–03137–0 (CSD) – ISBN 0–582–03136–2 (PPR)
1. Churchill, Winston, Sir, 1874–1965.
2. Prime ministers – Great Britain – Biography.
3. Great Britain – Politics and government – 20th century.
I. Title.   II. Series: Profiles in power
(London, England)
DA566.9.C5R56   1992
941.084′092 – dc20
[B]   91–46364   CIP

Set in Baskerville by 9P

Produced by Longman Singapore Publishers (Pte) Ltd.
Printed in Singapore

CONTENTS

PREFACE

'As the years pass', the editorial in the February 1991 Newsletter published by the Winston Churchill Memorial Trust sadly suggested,

> it is becoming increasingly evident that the average British citizen is less and less aware of Sir Winston Churchill – his life, his character, his contribution to this country and his legacy to the world. Personal memories of him are beginning to fade, and the school teaching of history or current affairs does not sufficiently cover his commanding role in national and world affairs in the first half of the 20th century. This lack of knowledge often proves embarrassing to Fellows not only during their Fellowship interviews, but also when their hosts enquire about the origins and aims of the Trust.

I was myself the grateful holder of a Travelling Fellowship from the Churchill Trust in 1990 and it enabled me to carry out an extensive programme of travel and interviews in many European countries. Since I met many modern historians in the course of my journey, it is perhaps not surprising that they possessed a greater knowledge of Churchill than the gloomy editorial feared. I also came across a new first translation into Magyar of Churchill's *The Second World War* – testimony to the fact that he still has something to say to the changing Europe of our time. Yet, there can be no doubt that the underlying contention of the editorial is correct. The name and face of Churchill are known all over the world, but the 'average British citizen' would find it difficult to come to a balanced appreciation of his greatness. He seems at once a contemporary and a remote figure.

This book will not supply 'the average British student' with everything that is to be known about Winston Churchill. In keeping with the objectives of this series, however, it seeks to give an outline of his career but, more fundamentally, to uncover what made possible that 'commanding role in national and world affairs in the first half of the 20th century'. His own attributes were given expression in an extraordinary empire in the final phase of its life. He lived long enough to experience the implications for his own creed which were inherent in its demise. He had an acute sense of the fluctuating fates of individuals and nations. Power could not be explained, but its achievement and its loss could be felt, both individually and nationally. Churchill did not seize power but he mingled with men who did. He had, indeed, at times a 'commanding role' but he was not so foolish as to suppose that even a man of power could shape the pattern of history. Meditation on his own career, however, with its unpredictable changes of fortune, suggested that there was a tide in the affairs of men which could be taken at the flood. Yet the victory which he helped to achieve had about it the smell of defeat. In his Indian Summer, it was not clear whether his long political journey led to the birth of a new Britain or merely the death of an old. There was plenty of evidence and plenty of doubt.

Professor Martin Pugh kindly performed an editorial task for the general editor, but mistakes or misjudgments are mine. This volume is dedicated to my former colleagues in Glasgow for their stimulus and friendship in the dozen years I spent with them. Doing history in a university over such a period of change has not been without some 'toil, tears and sweat' but happily it has been without blood and with more than an occasional element of laughter!

Chapter 1

WINSTON, THE HOUSE OF CHURCHILL AND THE DESTINY OF BRITAIN

. . .

HIS FATHER'S SON

Winston Churchill was born in the heart of England on St Andrew's Day, 30 November 1874. His place of birth was Blenheim Palace, the magnificent house built at Woodstock in rural Oxfordshire between the years 1705 and 1722. It was the gift of a grateful sovereign to John Churchill, first Duke of Marlborough, conqueror of the French and victor in the battle of Blenheim. Kings and princes from across Europe had to confess that even their palaces could not compare with the stately home of the Spencer Churchills, Dukes of Marlborough. The Victory column in the grounds of the palace reminded all visitors of a great English soldier's achievements – and of the rewards of success. John Churchill was Winston's ancestor. A baby born at Blenheim was liable to have an unusual perspective on life.[1]

The bells of Woodstock rang out in deferential celebration: baby Winston could be a future Duke of Marlborough. In manhood he might be guardian of the lake, the bridge and miles of glorious park. He would possess the power of a great English aristocrat, secure in his estates and preeminent in social position – there were only twenty dukes in the country. Like the 7th Duke, Churchill's grandfather, he might sit in the House of Commons before succeeding to the title. The borough of Woodstock offered an easy route to Westminster. Its voters were well-schooled in the notion that they should support the Churchill family. There might subsequently be a

1

ducal role in government, perhaps in a not too onerous capacity. Like the 7th Duke, and previous dukes, Winston might marry the daughter of a duke, a marquess or an earl. The House of Churchill would go on for ever. It never entered anyone's head that this aristocratic cherub would lead his country in a desperate struggle for survival. Hitler and Stalin, with whom he shared the world stage, ruthless and rootless wielders of power after the collapse of the old order in Europe, the order of aristocratic power and presumption, were inconceivable.

Even in Oxfordshire in the 1870s, however, the appearance of unchanging stability was a little deceptive. It was unlikely that the Marlboroughs would be swept away by invading peasants, but by the 1870s they were not insulated from the crisis of agriculture which, to greater or lesser degree, afflicted all great estates in the years of the 'Great Depression'. The story was one of falling rents and declining land values. There was no coal to be mined in Blenheim Park, but there was an alternative source of financial salvation on the far horizon. It was an Atlantic connection.[2]

The 7th Duke had two surviving sons (and six daughters). He came to feel that his heir was rather a 'disappointment' and that the continued restoration of the family's fortunes more might rest on his younger son, Lord Randolph, whose undistinguished Eton career had been followed by a period at Merton College, Oxford. In 1874 he had been elected to the House of Commons as MP for the 'family borough' of Woodstock – though there was increasing local opposition to the notion of a ducal 'nominee'. He had completed the statutory European tour and acquired experience of carousing. His walrus moustache made an impression on ladies. He was good with horses and words. The Prince of Wales admitted him to his circle. Combined, these attributes offered much promise, but he was the younger son of a relatively poor duke who had a rather large house and household to maintain.[3]

In April 1874 he married Jennie Jerome in the British Embassy Chapel in Paris. The Prince and Princess of Wales sent a generous present, and the prince's private secretary was his best man.The couple had met the previous summer at a Cowes Ball, but the subsequent negotiations for the marriage had not been straightforward. No previous Spencer

Churchill had married the daughter of an American stock-broker. Randolph's father noted that Jennie's father had been bankrupt once, and might become so again. On the other hand, he appeared to have a capacity for making (though also for spending) a great deal of money. At this particular phase in Jerome's financial cycle, however, he fortunately seemed comfortably placed, though from a ducal perspective he still gave every appearance of being a vulgar kind of man. The allowance which Mr Jerome and the Duke proposed to make naturally required careful consideration; and there was a possible offspring to be taken into account. The outcome permitted the lease of a house in Mayfair and the underwriting of the social life which would accompany it. Such provision, ample though it was, did not fully take into account the ambitions and activities of Randolph and Jennie.[4]

Blenheim, in all its splendour, was to be in the background throughout Winston Churchill's life, and even in death it was not out of sight. It is possible to see the tower of Bladon church from the palace. It was to Bladon churchyard that Winston was taken in 1965 for burial alongside his mother and father amongst the Churchill graves. Throughout his life he paid frequent visits and the most mixed memories came flooding back. He showed great skill in deciding that it would be sensible to propose to his future wife in Blenheim's Temple of Venus. He could not write a life of Marlborough without spending time at Blenheim. In the summer of 1938, he and Anthony Eden, newly resigned as Foreign Secretary, gloomily spent the evening on the terrace discussing the future of Europe. In 1947 he addressed a major Conservative rally in its grounds, sensing that he might yet turn the political tide in his favour.

Yet it was never his palace. Uncle George, who also had an American girl as his second wife, had a son, 'Sunny', who succeeded as 9th Duke in 1892. Three years later Sunny married Consuelo Vanderbilt. She brought with her from the United States an income of £20,000 a year and income from a fund of £500,000. Blenheim needed such resources. It also needed a son, apparently, to keep out the little upstart, Winston. The son was achieved but the marriage ended in divorce. Sunny's second wife, whom he married in 1921, was also American. In the event, the birth of a son meant that Winston was never to be Duke of Marlborough. If he had succeeded to the title he would never have become Prime Minister. The days were passing, indeed had passed, when a duke might realistically aspire to be Prime Minister. As a mere duke, of course, Winston would also not have been the subject of more biographical studies, large and small, than any other Englishman in the twentieth century. An accident to his cousin, and the future shape of his life would have been altered.

A paradox was therefore apparent from childhood: it was indisputable that as a Churchill he sprang from the 'ruling class' but only because he was the son of a younger son might he even aspire to be a real 'ruler'. Yet, as he grew up, it might be his aristocratic pedigree which would preclude such a possibility. The Second Reform Act, passed in 1867, had proved a risky 'leap in the dark'. In extending the franchise to give the vote to one in three adult males in England and Wales, the immediate effect had been to produce in 1868 a Liberal government presided over by Gladstone. It was that administration which had been defeated in the 1874 General Election in which Lord Randolph was elected to the House of Commons. At the age of seventy, Disraeli became Prime Minister. He had an opportunity to demonstrate that the Conservative Party could survive and flourish in the eyes of an extended electorate. It remained to be seen what contribution to this cause would be made by the dandy twenty-five-year-old member for Woodstock. Upon the outcome might depend the future career of baby Winston.

It was reasonable for the political world to suppose that Lord Randolph's career would be colourful and erratic. It was not reasonable for that world to predict that he would be dead at the age of forty-five. It did not know that he was already afflicted with syphilis. He struggled against this disease for the rest of his life, sometimes apparently with success, before it eventually killed him. While there is debate about the circumstances which produced the illness, there is little doubt now about its nature. The gravity of the complaint, which was sometimes suspected, may help to explain the impatience and unpredictability attaching to Lord Randolph's behaviour.

Churchill was certainly ambitious but he did not confine himself to politics, narrowly defined. He spoke only occasionally in the Commons and threw himself into a vigorous round of social engagements. In 1876 his conduct in a private matter involving the Prince of Wales and a lady brought him into disfavour at court. It led not to a duel with the prince in Rotterdam – an initial possible outcome – but to Randolph going to Dublin, in effect into 'exile', to act as unpaid secretary to his father who had recently been appointed Viceroy of Ireland. Whilst in Dublin, Irish politics occasionally interfered with hunting and the social life of the Viceregal Lodge. In addition, Lord Randolph spasmodically returned to London to make a few disconcerting speeches in the Commons. There was, for example, an assault in 1878 on the government's own County Government Bill which, he believed, attacked the right of property and undermined the independence of local self-government. He called it a radical and democratic measure which violated Tory principles. The attack was successful and confirmed the impression that Lord Randolph could be a coming man, particularly since the first steps were being taken to end the Churchills' banishment from court circles. It was not to be until 1884, however, that Randolph and the Prince of Wales sat down at table together again.

Gladstone and the Liberals won the 1880 General Election. Lord Randolph could not be said to have been particularly concerned with the welfare of his constituents over the preceding few years. He held his Woodstock seat only narrowly, despite the mobilisation of the Marlborough influence in his favour. The Liberal Cabinet looked so powerful and Northcote, the Conservative leader in the Commons, so weak. Randolph was impatient. Together with associates in the so-called 'Fourth Party' he embarked upon a series of parliamentary skirmishes which sometimes embarrassed his own side as much as the government. His speeches and his conversation sparkled with phrases that admirers found apt and incisive. His opponents recognised that he was rather a 'star' in the provinces. Disraeli died in 1881 and the subsequent arrangement whereby Lord Salisbury led the Tory Party in the Lords and Northcote in the Commons was not working well. Lord Randolph believed that he could manage a more effective Opposition, and increasingly behaved accordingly. He wrote to Northcote in 1883 declaring that in Parliament he had always acted on his own account and would continue to do so. He supposed that the results of such action had not been at all unsatisfactory.

It cannot be said, nevertheless, that the minutiae of policy, the delights of style or the intricacies of parliamentary strategy formed the daily diet on which young Winston was raised. He had a brother – who may not have been his father's child – born in 1880 and a devoted nanny, but his parents were aloof and detached. Neither Randolph nor Jennie allowed their lives to centre on their children. They were frequently apart and frequently ill in the early 1880s. In 1881 they despatched Winston to St George's School near Ascot. It was not a success. He was taken away by his mother three years later and sent to a small school in Brighton. He had been beaten and was rather frail. Lord Randolph came to Sussex, but he did not come to see his son. However, just ten, the boy by the seaside knew about General Elections. At the end of 1885 he wrote to his father wishing him success in the Birmingham seat which he was contesting, though he probably did not fully understand the campaign's significance.[5] The Third Reform Act of 1884, which extended the franchise to some two out of three adult males in England and Wales, was followed by a Redistribution Act. One of the boroughs to be disfranchised was Woodstock. Lord Randolph was forced to look for a new seat and, never one for half measures, announced that he would campaign against the venerable John Bright in Central Birmingham and, by implication, challenge the Liberal hegemony over the city's politics established by Joseph Chamberlain. Winston was sorry that the challenge failed but was relieved to know that Lord Randolph was elected instead for South Paddington, a safe seat.

In the space of a few years, Lord Randolph had become a 'name'. Politics became his passion. There was scarcely any manoeuvre, or perhaps the word is conspiracy, with which his name was not linked. He had managed to insinuate himself into the highest levels of the National Union of Conservative and Constitutional Associations, a body founded in 1867 which aspired to represent constituency opinion within the Conservative party. At the end of 1883 he had been present at the formation of the 'Primrose League'. In its initial conception its historian, Martin Pugh, sees the League as an extra-parliamentary 'Fourth Party' rather than an embryonic mass organisation. Banners and badges, however, feature prominently in its public activity. To what end was this hectic effort? Probably even Lord Randolph himself was not clear. He certainly had no respect for Northcote as party leader. Did he aspire to be party leader himself without further ado? The thought may have passed through his mind but even he might have supposed such an ambition premature. That left a relationship with Lord Salisbury in which the two men were both antagonists and partners. Salisbury saw Churchill as a popular figure who could undermine Northcote in the country in a way which he could not do himself. On the other hand, the National Union might place a demotic spanner in the workings of aristocratic government. In turn Churchill could make his own terms, or at least be in a strong position in a Salisbury government. An accord between the two men was reached in the summer of 1884. When a Conservative government was formed in June 1885 – the Liberals having been defeated in the Commons – Salisbury became Prime Minister and Lord Randolph became Secretary of State for India.

Salisbury was lugubriously pensive where Churchill was exuberantly garrulous but they were both reacting to the evident challenge to men of their order. The electoral changes of 1884–5 and the attack on 'corrupt practices' in an Act of 1883 threatened to remove the political role of the aristocracy. Salisbury had opposed the 1867 Reform Act and such were his forebodings then that he was somewhat surprised to find himself evidently still a major political figure nearly twenty years later. He thought hard and prayed hard. The British Constitution was a mixed constitution. If the Commons became dominant, would property be safe and if property was not safe could liberty survive? He was thinking of his country seat, Hatfield House, but not only of Hatfield House. The word 'democracy' – if it really implied that 'the people' should control government – was a rather uncomfortable one. Churchill, for his part, affected not to find 'democracy' alarming, provided the adjective 'Tory' was placed in front of it. In Birmingham in April 1884 he had urged his audience to 'Trust the People' and declared that he had no fear of democracy (by which, like most contemporaries, he meant not so much a system of government as 'the power of the people'). It should be the policy of the party to rally the people round the Throne and to unite the Throne with the people. He did not pray as hard as Lord Salisbury, but he also put in a good word for the Church of England, an institution which elevated the life of the nation and consecrated the acts of the State. Churchill appeared confident and Salisbury gloomy, but between them two representatives of 'old' families could perhaps conduct another skilful political adjustment in the century of aristocratic retreat.

Churchill's success in South Paddington had not been sufficiently repeated by Conservatives elsewhere in the country. However, the Liberals were in difficulties caused by Gladstone's announcement in opposition of his conversion to Home Rule for Ireland – a step which upset many in his own party. The early months of 1886 were full of extraordinary twists and turns in which Lord Randolph featured prominently. Adherence to steadfast principle will not explain the behaviour of any of the leading figures – Gladstone, Chamberlain, Salisbury and others – so we need not think of Lord Randolph's performance as exceptionally unprincipled. From his Dublin days onwards, he had made speeches in condemnation of coercion in Ireland and prized his Irish political contacts. Now, however, his opposition to Home Rule was fierce and even led him to speak favourably of the previously despised Ulster Tories. He was willing to 'play the Orange card' – that is to say identify with the Ulster opposition to Home Rule – and visit Belfast personally: it was inconceivable, he told his audience there, that the British nation would be so apostate as to hand over the Loyalists of Ireland to the domination of an Assembly in Dublin. Home Rule was simply an exercise to gratify the ambition of an old man in a hurry – Churchill's gift for a striking phrase had not deserted him. He floated the idea of a 'party of Union' which could fight against the impending disaster. Whatever its prospects, the Liberal Party had become the party of internal division, and Churchill had played a full part in encouraging the Liberal dissidents and causing the government to fall.

He had his reward by being made Chancellor of the Exchequer and Leader of the House in the government Salisbury formed after the Tories were successful in the General Election of July 1886. He was only thirty-six. Queen Victoria thought him 'mad and odd' but saw that his appointment could not be helped. She could not have suspected that this amazing man, who appeared to be successfully storming every political citadel, would be out of the government by the end of the year. Perhaps Lord Salisbury did. There were disagreements in Cabinet and the Prime Minister was amply provided with illustrations of Churchill's lack of judgment. It would not have been so bad if the Chancellor had refrained from pressing his views on foreign policy. His moodiness and arrogance were tolerable when relieved by his humour, but humour was increasingly absent. This was not the ideal spirit in which to approach the reconciliation of departmental claims in the framing of his first Budget. Churchill was uncompromising. He was determined to reduce expenditure and declared that he could not be responsible for finance if he had to yield to demands for increased spending. Epistolary exchanges followed.

The Duchess of Marlborough, who happened to be staying at Hatfield House, the Prime Minister's residence, awoke on the morning of 23 January to the news that her son had resigned and that his resignation had been accepted. It appeared that the Prime Minister was sanguine about this outcome. Prophecies that the government could not survive the loss of such a talented and popular figure proved false. At the beginning of 1887 Lord Randolph entered the political wilderness from which he never returned. Lord Rosebery, a man of comparable brilliance and comparable ultimate failure, was one of the few to be able to give him encouragement. In the short life that lay ahead of Churchill there were glimpses of former glories and flashes of the old inspiration but nothing could ultimately disguise his enfeebled decline.

These dramatic developments found Winston still at Brighton, no doubt bemused and bewildered by the turn of events. He was too young and his father too remote to register their lasting import. 'Trust the People' was the paternal injunction; Winston was sufficiently alert to another side of 'the people' to attempt an eleven-year-old's pen and ink sketch of the 'Trafalgar Square' rioters of 1886. Did those riots betoken the impending overthrow of the existing social order? In 1888 he started at Harrow – its position 'on the Hill' might make it healthier than Eton. In 1890 his mother complained that he worked in such a fitful and inharmonious way, though she was equally sure that he could accomplish anything he wished, if he really set his mind to it. Even the prospect of some Bechuanaland stamps promised by his father from

Johannesburg could not compensate for the lack of a real relationship with him. Strenuous efforts were made to get up Winston's French by sending him to France. On one visit he was able to compare the palace of Versailles with that of Blenheim – there was little to choose between them.

Churchill's generally dismal academic record at Harrow, however it may be explained or excused, did not encourage the notion of a university career. There was a fleeting but unsustained suggestion of 'the church' as a suitable career. The army increasingly seemed the answer and Winston returned to Harrow in September 1892 for his last term. Lord Randolph could not feel satisfied with the standard of his son's performance on getting into Sandhurst but it was only to be a little longer that his father's uncomprehending criticisms had to be endured.

Winston was just twenty at the time of his father's death. In one of his last letters Lord Randolph had pledged a great interest in his son's military career if he worked hard and demonstrated that he was wrapped up in his profession. Perhaps Lord Randolph had come to the conclusion that it was a better profession than the life of politics could ever be.[6]

It was not a conclusion that Winston was likely to draw. In August 1895 he was already expressing the view to his mother that 'the game of politics' was a fine one to play. He liked soldiering, and four years of healthy and pleasant existence, combined with responsibility and discipline, could do no harm, but he was already convinced that it was not his *métier* to be a soldier. He wanted to have a 'good hand' before plunging into politics. Meanwhile, he was already clear that he needed to broaden his mind. Thus far he had received what he called 'a purely technical education' and he lacked the polish which Oxford or Cambridge provided. He told his mother that at such institutions questions were studied with a rather higher object than 'mere practical utility'. He now had to supply that deficiency himself, perhaps with the help of a crammer. Political Economy and Modern History would be high on the list of subjects to be tackled. He would read Gibbon's *Decline and Fall of the Roman Empire* and Lecky on *European Morals*.

Such topics were at least different from the talk of 'horse' – 'in his every form & use' – which otherwise occupied most of the day. Not that Churchill objected to horses. When he passed his final examinations at Sandhurst (twentieth out of 130 cadets) his best marks had been for riding. Lady Randolph wrote to the Duke of Cambridge, the Commander-in-Chief of the Army, and Winston was formally commissioned and posted to the 4th Hussars stationed at Aldershot. He spent eight or nine hours a day in the saddle, and then there was polo. His mother was left in no doubt that being a cavalry officer was an expensive business. Winston realised that having a mother like Lady Randolph was also an expensive business. It was such a shame that 'we are damned poor'. Royal visitors to Aldershot wanted to meet Lord Randolph's son and he could have gone to a ball every night; but he did not.

All the time, however, an eye was kept on politics. The Unionist victory in the 1895 General Election was welcomed, though perhaps the new Cabinet was too strong and brilliant. The government might split on the question of Protection. Winston knew that acceptance of the merits of Free Trade was no longer automatic. Other countries were erecting tariffs. Lord Salisbury would need to steer the ship carefully, for any collision would mean destruction. Churchill had more reason than most young men of twenty to appreciate the hideous strength of personality. Yet without dynamic leadership parties could not prosper. In another letter to his mother at this time he attributed the 'ruin' of the Radical party to the absence of Gladstone's 'sustaining power'. As soon as he departed, the collapse ensued. In this instance, personality had imparted a fictitious strength – just as a fever animated a sick man. Perhaps this was a delicate analogy to draw so soon after his father's death, but there was no point in disguising the nature of things. It was because politics rested on the fickle impact of personality that it was a 'game'. But a player needed a 'good hand'. What was it? How could it be acquired?

Dukes of Marlborough and Marquesses of Salisbury had done nothing very special for generations and had then produced Lord Randolph and a Prime Minister. The Earl of Rosebery's father had sat in the Commons but although author of a helpful *Address to the Middle Classes upon the Subject of Gymnastic Exercises* he died from a heart attack before being able to pass on to his three-year-old son, the future Prime Minister, any wisdom on the secret of political success. Even so, underpinned by fresh wealth from his marriage to a

Rothschild heiress, the young Rosebery made his own way rapidly. His love of horse-racing, yachts and books demonstrated that there was no need to suppose that to be a politician one needed to regard politics as an austere self-contained 'profession'. Even amongst those sections of his party who did not keep horses, Rosebery's diverse activities enhanced his 'charisma'. He appeared to canter effortlessly to the Foreign Office and then briefly in 1894 to 10 Downing St in what turned out to be a disastrous Premiership. Rosebery lived until 1929 but he never held public office again. The parallel with Lord Randolph was alarmingly close. Their party allegiances were different, but it could appear that the aristocratic stable was producing horses which fell at early fences. Lord Salisbury, the incoming Conservative successor to Rosebery, kept his head down at Hatfield and did not repeal the death duties which he had so deplored when introduced by the previous Liberal government. His government was still aristocratic in tone but Salisbury himself had contributed to an erosion of the aristocracy's local power when in 1889 he had established county councils. Sensible Conservative peers, noting the way the political wind was blowing, instilled the virtues of compromise in their sons, though they did not all want to listen.

Predictably, a 'new man' like Joseph Chamberlain went about the business of training the next political generation with high bourgeois seriousness. He sent his son Austen to Rugby and Trinity College, Cambridge, where he read History and followed it up by serious lectures in Paris and Berlin. He did not think that his other son, Neville, either required or would benefit from similar exposure. Similarly, Stanley Baldwin's ironmaster/MP father sent his son to Harrow – he was seven years older than Winston – and then also to Trinity and also to read History. Cambridge history dons sedulously perpetrated the notion that their subject was a school for statesmen. Surely, their pupils would lead the country? On cue, Austen Chamberlain was elected unopposed to the Commons in March 1892. Stanley Baldwin, however, seemed to take things altogether less seriously and drifted off into the family business. Their respective fathers watched diligently over their welfare; a mixed blessing?

In contrast, Winston was on his own at Aldershot beyond the ken of Cambridge history dons. It is true that his mother took her parental duties more seriously after Randolph's death but she could not supply the political reflection he needed, though her social life and its ensuing intimacies could provide many contacts. His father of course could not help him, indeed, to his sorrow, had never helped him to make sense of politics. The paradox was that to the political world he was as yet simply his father's son. He could not escape this legacy but as yet could not find a way to handle it. He could not decide whether to emulate his father or seek to extricate himself from that example. Was Randolph a successful player or a failure? It is difficult to believe that Winston was unaware of the extent to which political circles still regarded the resignation of 1886 as enigmatic and probably absurd. The vague idea that Randolph was a bit 'mad' lingered on. It was also common knowledge that George, 8th Duke of Marlborough, Randolph's brother, was only forty-eight when he died in 1892. Contemporaries also knew that there was nothing in the life-style of Winston's parents which would have provided comfort and reassurance to counterbalance an instability which might have been hereditary. His own schoolmasters testified that Winston himself could be grumpy and uncooperative and even, on occasion, downright nasty. It is not surprising, given all these considerations, that Winston talked of 'waiting' before plunging into politics. It is equally not surprising that he did not really like the idea of waiting. Whatever else he had inherited, he had inherited impatience and, since he had joined the army, he may as well see the world.

· · ·

THE ARMY AND JOURNALISM

The span of Churchill's life (1874–1965) virtually coincided with the dramatic expansion and contraction of the British Empire. The 1870s and 1880s had seen a vast increase in the area of Africa under more or less direct British control. The context of British power was imperial. Before going to Sandhurst, Winston spent a little time in Switzerland and was intrigued by its various languages, but Switzerland was not a major element in the European balance. He did not undertake a 'grand tour' and did not know the great states of Europe at first hand. He was content to possess a modest historical knowledge picked up from school. There was a very good map of Europe on the wall of his Harrow classroom. It was beyond Europe that 'Greater Britain' was being born and where British destiny lay. Jennie Churchill may have become assimilated into the British scene, but she never forgot that she was an American. Her son had an itch to discover the New World for himself. When Winston announced that he intended to use his first extensive army leave to visit 'America and the Indies' she was required to furnish both finance to make the trip possible and introductions to significant people in New York. One of them, Bourke Cochran, caught his imagination as he expatiated on the benefits of eloquence.

Winston's first impressions, as he wrote to his brother Jack in November 1895, were that the United States was a very great country. What struck him most forcibly was that everything seemed to be judged from a practical standpoint. There seemed to be no such thing as reverence or tradition. Nor did government as such enjoy preeminent prestige – as he supposed it did in the United Kingdom. He formed the impression that in America first-class men were in the counting house and the less brilliant ones in the government. What did that say about where power was located? In an analogy which was by no means unique he pictured the American people as a great lusty youth – energetic, goodhearted, but vulgar. Overall, he found it difficult to reconcile his appreciation of the warm hospitality which was extended to him and his dislike of the raw vulgarity of the American press. There were refined and cultured people about, but they did not set the tone. His reactions perhaps reflected his own divided ancestry. There was a side of his character which relished the brashness of America. On the other hand, at least during a short visit, it was impossible to get his bearings. Near the apex of the British social structure himself, he found it difficult to believe that any society could function effectively without a clearly identifiable social hierarchy. These impressions, however, were not developed in any systematic fashion. They were the casual observations of a passing traveller whose real destination was Cuba, then still a Spanish possession.

Three years before the Spanish-American war of 1898, there was an insurrection on the island which Spanish forces were endeavouring to put down. He sent five 'Letters from the Front' which were published in the *Daily Graphic*. His

father had written for the newspaper on occasion so, once
again, he built on parental connections. Winston wrote clearly
and intelligently and came to firm views of his own. He was
not impressed by the actions of the guerillas. He could not
believe that wrecking trains and shooting from behind hedges
constituted acts on which progressive states were founded.
Cuban autonomy was impossible. The United States should
not force Spain to give up the island unless it was prepared to
take over responsibility for its welfare. He ended his last
article on a note of whimsy. If there had been English rather
than Spanish rule how much more prosperous Cuba would
have been. Cuban ponies would have been sent to Hur-
lingham and cricketers to Lords, Havana cigars would have
been exchanged for Lancashire cottons and Matanzas sugars
for Sheffield cutlery. He was not paid as much as his father
had been for comparable thoughts, but any payment was
welcome. And the final flourish indicated that Churchill had
a flair for his market.

He knew that his next destination, this time with the
Hussars, would be India. Just over a decade earlier, and the
year in which the Indian National Congress was founded, his
father had visited India. His schoolboy son naively enquired
'Are the Indians very funny?', but received no answer to the
question. Then, during his short tenure of the India Office,
Lord Randolph could claim the credit for the annexation of
Burma. Despite these links, Winston did not sail for India in
September 1896 with a sense of eager anticipation. Indeed,
he had tried to pull strings to get himself off, but to no avail.
He was conscious of India's distance from London and the
extent to which he would be removed from the centre of
power. Since the belief that he had to be a politician was
growing steadily stronger, he would have to take energetic
steps to prevent himself from slumping into a sterile exile.

His initial grumpiness was not helped by the fact that he
badly wrenched his shoulder attempting a premature personal
disembarkation at Bombay. It was to be an injury that
afflicted him for the rest of his life. In Bangalore, where the
regiment was stationed, he collected butterflies and played
polo. He formed a pronounced initial dislike of 'Anglo Indian
women' (i.e. British women in India), describing them privately as 'nasty'. The irony was that such vulgar creatures
supposed themselves to be great beauties. He was to make

15

only one exception among the British girls he met throughout his Indian years. He was determined from the start to find his life stupid, dull and uninteresting, and it lived up to his expectations. He was acutely conscious that he could appear just an insignificant young subaltern and he knew that he was not one. He would need to meet the people who ruled the country if his stay was to be of any value. He was reporting within a matter of weeks that his stay in India could not be long. His letters home display a continuing fascination with the possible permutations of British politics. He speculated, for example, on a possible combination between Lord Rosebery and Joseph Chamberlain which could sweep all before it. Polo tournaments offered a certain amount of excitement, as did the turf, but they remained distractions from the real game that Churchill wanted to play.

He relished letters but complained that only his mother wrote, and sometimes at no great length. Winston's were longer because they combined trivial news about polo with rehearsed declamations – almost 'state papers', expounding his views on political issues of the day. Lord Lansdowne, for example, Secretary of State for War, was fiercely criticised in one letter for advocating an increase in expenditure on the army. What Britain needed was an unequalled navy. Such a fleet would make it unnecessary to have an army for defence. An army corps or two would be sufficient for any enterprises in foreign countries that might prove necessary – outside Europe. He did not envisage any role in Europe. Otherwise, the British army's purpose was to provide a training ground for the army in India. He reiterated that sea power was the essence of the matter. A subaltern would be stranded and British power in India would be fatally weakened if sea communication could not be maintained. It was a judgment which reflected the reality of his own experience thus far. Whether right or wrong, it reflected too the premature firmness of his convictions. At the age of twenty-two he knew a stupid speech when he read one. His mother, detecting in her son the impatience of his father, urged him to read in the intervals of polo and military work. If he did not, when he was in politics and felt a want of knowledge, he would come to regret the time he had wasted. Winston saw the point and was supplied with a mixed bag of history, philosophy and political economy – while he sought to find a way of getting to Egypt. Books were all very well, but he might see active service and greater excitement there.

His reading was eclectic but solid. There were twelve volumes of Macaulay and almost as many of Gibbon. Jowett's translation of Plato's *Republic* temporarily lured him away from the latter. He found his literary tastes growingly rapidly and, if he only had the necessary Latin and Greek, stated that he would have left the army to take a degree in history, philosophy and economics. Unless a good opportunity presented itself of obtaining a seat in the House of Commons, there might after all be something to be said for staying in the army. He was reluctantly coming to see that it provided an excellent training. He asked now to be sent Adam Smith's *Wealth of Nations*. He recalled that Macaulay recommended Saint Simon's *Memoirs* and Gibbon recommended Pascal's *Provincial Letters*, so he asked for these volumes too. Laing's *Modern Science and Modern Thought* perhaps gave an overview of this important topic sufficient for general purposes.

One other work read at this time had a lasting impact on him: Winwood Reade's *The Martyrdom of Man*. He told his mother that it crystallised much of what he had for some time reluctantly believed. The author might have succeeded in proving Christianity false but Churchill was not persuaded that he had established that it was wise or expedient to say so. One day, perhaps, what he called 'the great laws of Nature' would be understood, and with it the human past and human destiny. It would then be possible to dispense with 'religious toys'. The 'crutch' of Christianity could at that point be put aside as men stood erect on the firm legs of 'reason'. He did not denounce 'religious toys'. They had agreeably fostered the development of mankind and it was disagreeable to be prematurely deprived of hopeful illusions. A little later, in correspondence with his clergyman Harrow headmaster, who had become Bishop of Calcutta, he firmly stated his opposition to Christian missions.

He gave little sign of wrestling with the God of the Christians or of taking seriously what the Church of England thought a Church might be. He continued to believe that the young benefited from a religious teaching provided that it was unsectarian. In schools, the Bible (without comments) and *Hymns Ancient and Modern* (with a few exceptions) would suffice. This religious instruction should not be placed in the hands of any sect, the Church of England included, for each was partisan. It should be in the hands of secular instructors appointed by government. More generally, he took the common-sense view that if a church was 'established' then naturally it was for the government to insist on effective control: 'who pays the piper calls the tune', as he put it. England did indeed have an 'established' church and as churches went it was not a bad one, but it could not change its doctrines without undermining the constitution.

These historical and religious notions, formulated in the intervals between polo matches by a detached Englishman in the heart of South India in the year of Queen Victoria's diamond jubilee, lodged in his mind for a lifetime. He absorbed leading themes into his discourse with remarkable facility, but neither in Bangalore nor subsequently were they subjected to the scrutiny and criticism that might have taken place at a university. There was excitement in the reading but there was neither the time nor the environment to explore ideas in their more detailed application and implication. Paradoxically, perhaps, it was the very absence of a critical context which allowed his newly-released enthusiasm for language to flow. It might never have burst forth with such richness in academic circumstances. And even at this time Churchill was aware of the dangers. Of all people, it was Cecil Rhodes, the South African mining magnate, who pointed out a 'mental flaw' in young Winston, a flaw which, in a letter to his mother in April 1898, Winston freely admitted to. It sounded very terrible to say so, he knew, but it was a fact that he did not so much care for the principles he advocated as for the impression which his words produced and the reputation they gave him.

Certainly, he went to very great lengths to reflect on oratory and identified certain cardinal elements. Amongst them were correctness of diction; it was always necessary to choose the best possible word. Thinking of John Bright, he believed that the great speakers, except when addressing highly cultured audiences, employed short, homely words of common usage. The words should then be arranged so that a rhythm was created. The argument should then move to a climax and should be helped along its path by the apt use of analogy. The orator was the embodiment of the passions of the multitude.

But to what end was all this elaborate word play? Here indeed was a problem with which to wrestle. What was the actual content of politics? What did a politician actually need to know, whatever his ability to make use of that knowledge? Once again, he tackled the question seriously, though his method is not without its ludicrous aspects. His mother had been prevailed upon, with some reluctance because of bulk and expense, to send out copies of the *Annual Register*, that valuable compendium of useful information. It was from this source that he intended to discover the detailed parliamentary history of the previous hundred years. He did not read an account of a debate in the *Register* until he had formulated his own opinion on paper. He then read what had been said and rewrote his own ideas accordingly. In this way he hoped to develop a logical and consistent mind. Of course, he recognised that the *Annual Register* was only good for facts, but the 'power of facts' was undeniable and inescapable. So, solemnly, Churchill wrote out his thoughts on such matters as 'The Endowed Schools Act Amendment Bill', 'The Burial Question' and 'The Judicature Amendment Act'. He confessed to ignorance of this latter act's details, but enunciated a notion of very general applicability. Modern principles should be 'clothed with the picturesque garments of the past'. Any ceremony or rite which encouraged reverence, sentiment or affection should be preserved in progressive times, though such considerations must not be predominant.

Did this voluminous dialogue with the House of Commons, carried on in the heat of India, produce a 'policy' of the kind that parties affected to possess? Churchill does not seem to have been very sure. Certainly there were votes of censure passed privately in the Bangalore cantonment. Lord Salisbury's 'obstinate boorishness' was identified without approval, so were Balfour's 'pusillanimous vacillations', Lansdowne's 'ridiculous "reforms"' and Curzon's 'conceit'. Transported to the House of Commons, there were no lengths to which Winston would not have gone in opposing the government. Indeed, in March 1897 he wrote to his mother that he was Liberal in all but name. Were it not for Home Rule – to which he would never consent – he would enter Parliament as a Liberal. Somewhat reluctantly, therefore, he would range himself under the standard of Tory Democracy. That creed implied reform at home. He would support: the extension of the franchise to every male; universal education; equal establishment of all religions; wide measures of local self-government; an eight hours working day; payment of MPs (if they requested it); a progressive income tax. He was clear, however, that such changes could only be contemplated domestically. East of Suez it was impossible to apply 'democracy'. India would need to be governed on old principles and the colonies 'federated' for defence and commercial purposes. As far as European politics was concerned, Britain should keep 'absolutely unembroiled' and indeed isolated. Such a combination of policies would have the gratifying outcome of ensuring peace and power abroad and prosperity and progress at home.

These were policies of a kind. It was not certain that they expressed convictions. Indeed, Churchill had to admit that he very rarely detected genuine emotion in himself and normally lacked 'a keen sense of necessity or of burning wrong or injustice' such as would make him 'sincere'. It could be, therefore, that politics was an activity without values. The conquest of power could be achieved by technique and application. There was no such a thing as 'right' or 'wrong', everything was a matter of expediency and presentational skill. Churchill may have been driven to think so sometimes, but some kind of moral discourse could not be excluded. Concerning the British government's reaction to the Cretan uprising of 1897, for example, he claimed to be looking at the question 'from the point of view of right & wrong' whereas Lord Salisbury considered it from the standpoint of profit and loss. There is little evidence, however, that Churchill was interested in subjecting 'right' and 'wrong' to philosophical scrutiny. That was not how his mind operated. Nevertheless, the apparent arbitrariness of political preferences did give him some anxiety. He drew some comfort from his belief that he did not live in the days of 'Great Causes'.

In any event, he had more immediate problems to worry about. The chief of them was money. A comprehensive preparation for a political career was pointless without some prospect of financial independence to support it. As things stood, Winston and his mother vied with each other in financial improvidence and expenditure. Each hoped to rein the other in, but could offer each other no convincing personal example as to how such things might be done. There were promises of improvement of life, but nothing could obscure the fact that additional income was required. It fell to Winston to provide that income. He knew very well that without money he could not advance to power. It was not merely that an MP received no salary, but that political life, on the grand scale that Winston appeared to envisage, entailed a host of expenses. It was inconceivable that he would launch himself into business, but it was already clear that his passion for words could find a profitable outlet in journalism. Disraeli, in not dissimilar circumstances, had turned to novel-writing and Churchill could seek to emulate him, at least in this respect.

The material for journalism would be provided by being present during as many military campaigns as, by one means or another, he could achieve. In the first place, in late 1897, he managed to get an appointment as a 'press correspondent' with the so-called Malakand Field Force which was in action in the North-West Frontier region of India. Reports of this expedition were published in the *Daily Telegraph*, anonymously – Churchill was disappointed because the purpose of writing was to bring his personality before the electorate. His mother had again been busy on his behalf.

However, he was soon on active service in circumstances of rapidly accelerating danger. The skirmishes in which he was involved were short but intense. He knew what it was to see men die around him. He placed himself deliberately and conspicuously in exposed positions because, amidst the danger, he never forgot the purpose of his presence. It might be foolish to ride along the skirmish line while others were taking cover but he was playing for high stakes. Given an audience, as he put it, there was no act which was too daring or too noble. He claimed to be of an adventurous disposition and to be determined to enjoy himself, not so much in spite of the risks he was running as because of them. In this light it was a little disappointing only to be 'mentioned in despatches', but that was better than nothing. All the time, he was thinking ahead. The fact of having seen service with British troops while still a young man would give him more weight politically. He believed that it would also improve his prospects of gaining popularity back home in Britain. It seemed that there was nothing he undertook which did not have these objectives in mind.

The same applied to his plan hastily to transform his newspaper correspondence into a book – which appeared in the spring of 1898 under the title *The Story of the Malakand Field Force*.[7] Winston found the experience of putting this book together exhilarating and, despite problems in its production, was pleased with its reception. He was pleased with the publicity he received, not to mention the worthwhile financial benefit. 'Everyone is reading it', wrote the Prince of Wales to the author, and he only heard it being spoken of with praise. Supposing that Winston really aspired to a notable military career, the prince added, he would surely have the chance of winning a VC on some future occasion. He also added his view that Churchill should stick to the Army for a time before adding MP to his name. In circles in which the prince did not perhaps move, however, the author of the book was not beyond criticism. Needless to say, Churchill had offered some opinions on the general strategy to be pursued in the mountainous districts and there were those who wanted to know by what right a young serving officer expressed his views publicly. How did he get such generous leave?

Such criticism did not bother Churchill. Before the book's publication, he had written that its reception would enable him to measure the chances of his future success in the world. He was distinctly encouraged by the outcome and set about pushing and shoving, as he put it, to gain permission to be with Kitchener, the British commander in the Sudan. The reluctant Kitchener eventually crumbled before the combined efforts of his mother, the Prince of Wales and the Prime Minister. Churchill called on the latter in person while on a visit to London. In early August 1898 he advanced up the Nile to join a new regiment, the 21st Lancers. He also had a contract to write articles for the *Morning Post*. Once again, he explained to his mother, what drove him on was a sense of adventure. He did not flinch from whatever might lie ahead, even though he did not accept the Christian or any other form of religious belief. The Battle of Omdurman lay ahead.

Churchill emerged from the battle without a hair of his horse or a stitch of his clothing being touched, though the regiment's casualties were not light. He was glad to have added the experience of a cavalry charge to his military repertoire and wrote lively accounts for the *Morning Post*. He knew, however, that Kitchener resented his presence and would certainly grant him no further facilities. Churchill grudgingly referred to him as a great general, but he was certainly not a great gentleman. There was no further place for Winston in the Sudan and he returned to the 4th Hussars via England. The next battle that lay ahead was the inter-regimental polo tournament where his ferociously unpredictable hitting unexpectedly produced three goals in the final.

When he first arrived in India he had lamented that he had little contact there with the great men who shaped events. That was beginning to change. He was invited to spend a week in Calcutta with Lord Curzon, the new Viceroy, as a result of which each man formed a somewhat more favourable impression of the other. Even so, the prospect of settling down to the routine life of Bangalore, after so much recent excitement, was hardly enticing. He was working on his account of the Sudan campaign against the Dervishes which was to be published under the title of *The River War*, a task in which he received no encouragement from Kitchener or his entourage. Lord Cromer, who represented British authority in Egypt, proved more helpful when Churchill came to Cairo on his way back to England.

This voyage home in March 1899 was unlike all the others he had made. He had just decided to resign his commission in the army. It was as rash a decision as any he had made thus far, though not an unexpected one. By one means or another, he had managed to fit in first-hand experience of battle during his brief period of service. There was nothing to be gained from lingering longer in the army. It was true that he had no reliable regular profession to embark upon but, as he explained, far from the army being a source of income, he was more out of pocket the longer he stayed in. He believed he could live more cheaply and earn more as a writer, special correspondent or journalist. It was a risk, but he specialised in risks.

It was important to press on with *The River War*, both for what it would earn and what he hoped it would do for his reputation, but it was not his only literary project. Since 1897 he had been working, off and on, at a novel which had the working title of 'Affairs of State'. It was serialised in 1899 and appeared under the title of *Savrola* in early 1900. Its characters had vaguely 'Austro-Bulgarian' names and the story, predictably, was political. Savrola, the hero, was the leader of a popular movement against the autocratic regime of President Molara. He was a philosopher-orator who was clearly the greatest force in his country's politics, but who worried about Fate. He could communicate with the soul of his people but was he a medium or a mentor? Savrola subscribed to a 'sad cynical evolutionary philosophy'. So did Churchill. The novel was generally well-received, but few supposed that Winston was really a novelist.[8]

The River War had appeared a few months earlier. Quite apart from its other merits, it was testimony to Churchill's power of work. It was published in two volumes and devoted nearly a thousand pages to this episode in the Sudan. The author's power of exposition was generally praised. He did not, however, restrict himself to narrative description but expressed some forceful criticisms – of Kitchener amongst others. The arrogance of the youthful author in this respect did not excite universal admiration. The *Daily Mail* felt that a century hence it might seem excessive to devote so many pages to what would appear a mere episode, though it thought the book an astonishing achievement. On balance, reviewers were favourable. No one could fail to spot that its author had read a good deal of Gibbon and Macaulay, but Churchill was also beginning to have a voice of his own.

It might have made an even bigger impact had it not appeared in the very month that another war occupied the headlines. Indeed, on the day of publication, Churchill was on board ship bound for South Africa where the Boer War had just begun. He had obtained an assignment as correspondent of the *Morning Post* with a substantial fee. Even so, he could not resist the possibility of some military glory and acquired a commission in the Lancashire Hussars. It did not take long for the ambiguity of his status to become contentious. He obtained a place on an armoured train which would take him close to the fighting in Natal. It was derailed and ambushed. Churchill was drawn into the ensuing melée and subsequently taken prisoner of war. The details of the affair are to some extent disputed. Was he a non-combatant journalist or a soldier? There was also to be some controversy surrounding the precise circumstances of his subsequent escape from imprisonment in Pretoria. Had he been right to go solo when the original plan had been that three men should make their escape together? What is not contentious is that when he finally reached Durban on 23 December 1899 he was the hero the Empire was looking for after a series of severe setbacks earlier in the month. He knew it. He willingly complied with demands for a speech.

He immediately followed up his words by action, joining the South African Light Horse while continuing to serve as a war correspondent. He remained in South Africa for another six months and managed to be present at most of the vital encounters during this period. He moved rapidly from place to place and his despatches excited much interest. He could not see too much fighting. He plunged into a fresh book on his own experiences, *London to Ladysmith via Pretoria* (which was to be followed by a sequel, *Ian Hamilton's March*), and received the gratifying news that his escape and the publicity it had received had boosted the sales of his other books. He was beginning to make serious money but was so busy that he had little opportunity to spend it. The question now had to be faced: when was it time to come home and begin the serious business of politics, for all that he had done so far was merely a preparation for power?

Even during his leaves home from India, he had started to make himself known. In the summer of 1897 at Claverton Manor outside Bath he addressed his first public meeting. He believed that there was a rising tide in favour of Tory Democracy and contrasted its benefits with the 'dried-up drain-pipe of Radicalism'. A year later, he successfully addressed a packed meeting in Bradford and hints were given that he should keep his eye on the Central Division. After this speech, Winston felt great relief. He was confident that with practice he could obtain great power on the public platform. His speech impediment was not the obstacle he sometimes feared it might be.

In the event, however, it was a Lancashire rather than a Yorkshire seat that Churchill first contested. In the summer of 1899, between returning from India and embarking for South Africa, he fought a by-election at Oldham, where one of the sitting MPs, a Conservative, had died. However, Churchill did not retain the seat for the government but was reassured by Balfour, amongst others, that all would come right before long. Therefore, despite all the excitement of events in South Africa, Churchill did not want to be out of the country when a General Election was held. The capture of Pretoria seemed to suggest that the war was virtually over – though this assumption proved incorrect – and Churchill sailed for home. By the time he had landed at Southampton on 20 July he had finished what was to be the last of his four war books. All sorts of people wanted to meet this best-selling celebrity.[9]

Although he received approaches from other constituencies, Churchill soon headed for Oldham. The local band played 'See the Conquering Hero Comes' amidst huge crowds and in a festive atmosphere. In fact, however, when the General Election did come in early October Churchill had a stiff fight before he conquered. There was no doubt that the willingness of Joseph Chamberlain, the Colonial Secretary, to come and speak for him helped him to victory in the so-called 'khaki' election. Emotions were running high and South Africa was to the fore. Churchill was delighted with the outcome but even in the moment of victory recognised that Oldham, in the long term, was not a secure seat. In thanking Lord Salisbury, the Prime Minister, for his congratulations, Winston stated that it was clear to him from the figures that nothing but personal popularity arising out of what he optimistically called 'the late South African War' had carried him in.

In the short term, however, he was where he had wanted to be ever since he had first thought about politics. He was still only twenty five and he had reached Westminster. In January 1898 he had written to his mother from Bangalore in these terms:

> In Politics a man, I take it, gets on not so much by what he *does*, as by what he *is*. It is not so much a question of brains as of character & originality . . . Introduction – connections – powerful friends – a name – good advice well followed – all these things count – but they lead only to a certain point. As it were they ensure admission to the scales. Ultimately – every man has to be weighed – and if found wanting nothing can procure him the public confidence.[10]

Introduction, connections, powerful friends and a name had indeed helped to admit him to the scales, though he could also feel some satisfaction and gain some confidence from his own energetic exertions. Publicity, even notoriety, had swept him into the House of Commons; but he was realistic enough to understand that power rested on a public confidence which he had not yet achieved. The weighing time had indeed arrived.

. . .

NOTES AND REFERENCES

1. M. Beard, *English Landed Society in the 20th century*, London, 1989, pp.14–17.
2. D. Cannadine, *The Decline and Fall of the British Aristocracy*, London, 1990, and J.V. Beckett, *The Aristocracy in England 1660–1914*, Oxford, 1986, contain ample information on the fate of great families.
3. R.F. Foster, *Lord Randolph Churchill: A Political Life*, Oxford, 1981. R. Rhodes James, *Lord Randolph Churchill*, London, 1959.
4. Peregrine Churchill and Julian Mitchell, *Jennie. Lady Randolph Churchill*, London, 1974.
5. Randolph S. Churchill, *Winston S. Churchill*, Volume I *Youth. 1874–1900*, London, 1966, p. 69.
6. Randolph S. Churchill, *Winston S. Churchill*, Volume I Companion Part 1 1874–1896, London, 1967, p. 466. Martin Gilbert, *Winston S. Churchill* London, 1991, adds more detail (pp.19–34)) on aspects of Churchill's life at Harrow to supplement that offered in the volume on his *Youth* by Randolph Churchill, *op.cit.*
7. Winston S. Churchill, *The Story of the Malakand Field Force*, London, 1898.
8. Winston S. Churchill, *The River War*, London, 1900; *Savrola*, London, 1900. Paul Addison, 'The Political Beliefs of Winston Churchill', *Transactions of the Royal Historical Society*, Fifth Series vol. 30, 1980, pp. 30–5. Maurice Cowling, *Religion and Public Doctrine in Modern England*, Cambridge, 1980, pp. 287–92.
9. Winston S. Churchill, *London to Ladysmith via Pretoria*, London, 1900; *Ian Hamilton's March*, London, 1900.
10. Winston S. Churchill, Volume I Companion Part II, London, 1967, pp. 863–4.

Chapter 2

THE PARLIAMENTARY
PURSUIT OF POWER

. . .

TORY MP

In Bangalore, Churchill had planned and speculated about
his career in British politics in considerable detail, but he had
never dreamed of Oldham. Most of its voters were probably
working-class, despite the existing franchise. The grim concerns of a textile town just north of Manchester had no place
in his consciousness. He was familiar at first hand with large
tracts of the British Empire, but he was not familiar with
large tracts of Britain. Before his election for Oldham, he had
only been to the North of England on a couple of occasions.
Scotland was *terra incognita*. This young hero of the North-
West Frontier, the Upper Nile and the South African veldt
knew nothing of the world of textile mills and engineering
workshops, or indeed of shops in general. The men who
supported Oldham Athletic knew nothing about polo.
Churchill's smooth round face and delicate hands contrasted
clearly with theirs. Yet Churchill was not physically impressive, being only five foot six-and-a-half inches tall. He did not
naturally stand out – which perhaps explains his enthusiasm
for dressing up and for hats in particular. One of his biggest
regrets on leaving the army was that he would no longer be
able to wear the uniforms in which he had delighted. It
remained to be seen how far, if at all, the new member and
his constituents influenced each other.

The Oldham triumph would almost certainly require him
to formulate what might be called policies. His Liberal

opponents were furious that the campaign had centred on Churchill's 'undoubted physical courage' rather than upon the political issues involved. The exigencies of the campaign had forced him to make statements on mysterious aspects of Church politics, but now he would have to be explicit on other general issues. Even so, he refused to accept that physical courage had no bearing on the life of politics. He still believed that men voted for real men rather than for mere embodied programmes – he had not altogether given up the idea of writing on Garibaldi or Lincoln, men who exemplified this truth.

The word 'men' is used advisedly. Since his schooldays, his society had very largely been male. In 1897, in his commentaries on the *Annual Register* he declared his unswerving opposition to the ridiculous movement to give women the vote. If that were ever to occur it would ultimately be necessary to allow women to sit at Westminster and that would be disastrous, since 'Once you give votes to the vast numbers of women who form the majority of the community, all power passes to their hands'.[1] In the interval he had not met any woman who caused him to contemplate this prospect with anything other than horror. He had a kind of attachment for Miss Pamela Plowden, whom he had met in India, but it appeared that there were more interesting things to do than to cultivate it. It was clear to him that women still did strange things. His mother, for example, had just married his own contemporary, George Cornwallis-West. Miss Plowden was to marry the Earl of Lytton, whose sister was an ardent advocate of votes for women.

All his recent experience had confirmed him in the belief that British destiny could never be severed from the British Empire. Run of the mill decisions in domestic politics rested ultimately on this bedrock. When he first went to India, his headmaster had told him that he would be 'a witness of the most interesting administrative work that has ever been done among men'.[2] On inspection, Churchill agreed and urged foreigners to come and see for themselves what a remarkable work was being achieved by the British in India. In his maiden public speech at Bath in 1897, Jubilee year, he was scathing on the subject of those who believed that the British Empire had reached the height of its glory and power and would begin to decline. He dismissed such people as 'croak-

29

ers'. On the contrary, the vigour and vitality of the race would enable the British to carry out their mission of bearing peace, civilisation and good government to the uttermost parts of the earth. That was the ringing language he liked. He was not one to subject the imperial experience to cost-benefit analysis. His faith in 'our race & blood' had been much strengthened by his experience of the men in the 21st Lancers in the Sudan.

Even so, at the beginning of the new century there was some cause for concern. There was no one more proud of the British Empire, but he could see no gain in a possible conflict with Russia. Just as patriotism could shade into cant, so Imperialism could sink to Jingoism. The British did bring a superior order, but at a price, a price which could include their own corruption. On the North-West Frontier he knew that in warfare no quarter was ever asked or given, but felt that in the nature of things a permanent settlement was still far off and there would be a great deal of killing to come. In the Sudan, he had been depressed by the behaviour of its civilised conquerors in digging up the corpse of the Mahdi and carrying his head to Cairo. He was also acutely conscious that there had been far too much initial optimism concerning the military struggle in South Africa. It was no less a person than the Colonial Secretary who, in thanking Churchill for *The River War*, remarked in March 1900 that 'our extended Empire renders us liable to a strain on our military resources for which we are insufficiently prepared'.[3]

It was in this context that his thoughts again turned to his mother's country. He conceded that the diplomatic manners of the United States were odious, but what appealed to him about Americans was the fact that they acted – lately in the Spanish-American war. He declared in 1898 that one of his political principles would be to promote good understanding between the English-speaking communities. The Colonial Secretary, who now had an American wife, also seemed to share this viewpoint. Churchill's mother played her part by launching what turned out to be a short-lived *Anglo-Saxon Review* with the same general aims. Her son objected to the motto 'Blood is thicker than water' on the grounds that it had long ago been relegated to the pothouse music hall. Nonetheless, the 'Yankee Marlborough' approved of the attempt to bring together the two elements in his ancestry and spoke approvingly of the 'English-speaking people'.

Churchill's disdain for cheap Imperialist productions for thousands of vulgar people did not altogether square with his own activity in the months that followed his election. The notion that it would be prudent to buy a house in the constituency never crossed his mind. Instead he embarked on a tour of discovery in Britain, giving twenty-nine lectures throughout the kingdom on his South African experiences and publications. It was followed by a similar trip to the United States and Canada. These activities certainly helped Churchill's finances. From Toronto on New Year's Day 1901 he proudly reported to his mother that he had earned £10,000 without any capital in less than two years. A politician of his ambition needed such underpinning. He was in Winnipeg when he heard the news of the death of Queen Victoria. The following month, at the beginning of a new reign, he made his first speech in the Commons.

The new member did not seem a stranger in the House of Commons, though few MPs knew him well. He could not escape the fact that he was seen as his father's son. He was a very junior young man but seemed to suppose from the outset that he was on a par with such major figures as Balfour or Chamberlain. The Conservative Party was anxious to make use of Churchill's fame but he himself was not sure that he wanted to be used. Coming into parliament in the way he had done, he had not become enmeshed in obligations to the party organisation. From the outset, he contrived a position of some independence. The government itself was reconstructed after the election and it was likely that Lord Salisbury would make way for his nephew, Balfour, before too long. The change took place in July 1902, by which time Churchill had already made a name for himself, particularly because of his attacks on Brodrick at the War Office who sought to expand the Army by providing it with three home-based army corps. Churchill played a substantial part in defeating the proposal. He maintained his belief in a supreme navy. In general, his presence and contributions were received with a mixture of amusement, envy and apprehension. There was a nervous excitement about him – it was noted that he could not sit still – which was both worrying and stimulating. It was scarcely surprising that Balfour did not offer Churchill a post in his government – but the future course of events might have been very different if he had.

Churchill spent a good deal of time in the company of the so-called 'Hooligans', a small group of Tories around Lord Hugh Cecil, one of the sons of the Prime Minister. They all liked talking a great deal. Lord Hugh's voice was reputedly like the quacking of a sad but melodious duck. Churchill quacked back effectively. One of the drawbacks about Lord Hugh was that he believed that right was separated from wrong by a bottomless gulf and perpendicular cliffs.[4] Fond of him though Churchill remained, he was not likely to be a companion on the way to power. Lord Hugh, for his part, had detected a 'lamentable instability' in his new companion. The skirmishing of the Hooligans brought back memories, for some, of the former 'Fourth Party' in which Lord Randolph had been active alongside the new Prime Minister, Balfour. In his new position, however, Balfour came to understand how difficult it was to keep a party together. After May 1903, when Chamberlain publicly stated his belief in Tariff Reform, with attendant imperial preferences, the Prime Minister struggled to find a formula to maintain unity. What would Churchill do?

It was not inconceivable that he might be attracted by Chamberlain's new course. Lord Randolph in the past had wobbled somewhat on the subject of 'fair trade'. In fact, Winston moved in precisely the opposite direction, perhaps because speeches he had made in his constituency convinced him that his voters were still wedded to Free Trade. He himself stated his opposition to a 'self-contained Empire' and wrote to the Prime Minister in strong terms. His absolute loyalty would be given to Balfour in an attempt to preserve the Free Trade policy and character of the Tory Party, but any alternative course would compel him to reconsider his position in politics. The protective system would involve commercial disaster and 'the Americanisation of English politics'. Naturally, Balfour gave nothing away in his reply.

Within days, Churchill was writing to the Leader of the Opposition, Campbell-Bannerman, suggesting joint action to maintain Free Trade. Contact with Liberals was not a novelty. Almost from the moment of entering the Commons, Churchill had sought to explore the possibility of a 'middle party', though since Lord Rosebery was involved in the discussions a lifetime of indecision probably lay ahead. Now things had become urgent. In an article, Churchill pointed to the difficulty in which moderate and reasonable people (that is to say people like himself) found themselves. As Balfour tried to square the circle, in a series of puzzling moves, Churchill's departure to the Liberals grew steadily more likely. His speeches became ever more critical. Balfour was subjected to withering, carefully-prepared insults. The final severance, however, took place in stages for, although the Conservative whip was withdrawn in January 1904, it was not until May that he moved to a seat on the Opposition side of the House. He was now revealed as a fully-fledged English Liberal who, in his own words, hated the Tory Party, their men, their words and their methods.

Tory MPs found this hatred neither plausible nor tolerable. They shunned him personally and savaged him politically. There had been criticism in the past, as for example from Lord Lindsay, the Tory Whip, that Churchill had been 'spouting as usual in his vain and priggish manner'. Now, however, Churchill's desertion to the enemy brought vitriolic attacks on his conduct. The criticisms which accompanied his arrival in the Commons were muted no longer: Winston was vain, brash, bumptious and untrustworthy; in short, in a description attributed to King Edward, he was a 'born cad'.[5]

. . .

LIBERAL MP

So why did Churchill take this momentous step? The direct answer appears to be because of his belief in Free Trade. He claimed that it would be disastrous to lay the foundations of a democratic empire upon the protective taxation of food. The British Empire should not be walled off like some medieval town. However, few could believe that the rhetorical rehearsal of Cobdenism, which Churchill offered up and down the country, constituted a sufficient explanation for his conduct. He was surely fleeing from the Conservatives because there was no prospect of rapid advance under Balfour and because he sensed that the pendulum was swinging against them? If he was to link himself with the party which might dominate the next decade he could not wait until a Liberal victory at the next General Election. He had to act at once and if his departure was accompanied by bitter Tory attacks his passage into the heart of Liberalism might be smoothed. Of course, Churchill protested his sincerity and sought to maintain personal relationships with those with whom he was publicly brawling, but one would not expect him to claim ambition for office as his motive.

Whatever interpretation be placed upon his action, it was obviously a gamble. The Conservative Party was in disarray but, since the Liberals were in little better shape internally, it might yet achieve victory at the next General Election. In addition, Churchill had to deal with the criticism that to express hatred for a party so soon after being elected under its auspices was somewhat precipitate. Either the initial decision or the latest decision indicated a lack of judgment. The way to answer such criticism was to press ahead with the biography of Lord Randolph on which he was already engaged.

There was a poignancy and delicacy in a portrait of the father by the son at this particular juncture. Winston took enormous pains in the narration of what was portrayed as a great tragedy, though he showed a convenient talent for compartmentalising his material and overlooking certain problems. When the book was published in January 1906 it was to critical acclaim. It also sold well. Here was a work way beyond conventional piety. Lord Randolph's latest biographer has rightly drawn attention to the way in which Winston chose to ignore or to place in misleading context certain materials which were open to him. It is scarcely surprising that this should have been the case, for the two stout volumes contained a thesis which was barely disguised. Lord Randolph's supposed discovery of 'Tory Democracy' was emphasised. His espousal of this cause had prevented the Tory Party from slipping down into the gulf of departed systems. He had been instrumental in sustaining Tory support among the masses. Without his efforts, British politics would have rested upon social rather than political divisions. He had ensured that the country's institutions continued to be esteemed among the masses of the British people. His resignation was testimony to his consistency, not his waywardness. That was the message his son needed to convey.

In the month that saw the publication of the biography, Churchill returned to the House of Commons as Liberal MP for Manchester North West – a constituency which had returned a Conservative unopposed at the previous election. He was swept along in the tide which produced a large Liberal majority across the country. Winston claimed that the Tories had been overtaken by the irretrievable catastrophe which his father had always dreaded and sought to prevent. The old gang had allegedly been preserved in power by Lord Randolph's efforts, yet they had treated him ungratefully. Churchill was delighted that circumstances had enabled him to break with the Conservative Party while still young. He would now devote himself to 'the popular cause'. Such an interpretation enabled him to defend the consistency of his own conduct, for the logic of 'Tory Democracy' pointed to Liberalism.

Yet there was more than a suspicion that any party was an inadequate vessel. In the peroration which closed the biography, Churchill appealed to that 'England' which existed 'beyond the well-drilled masses who are assembled by party machinery' and to wise men who gazed without self-deception at the failings of both political parties.[6] Even at the moment of his joining the Liberal Party it was only grudgingly that he accepted the need for any kind of disciplined party. He was not unique in this reservation. In the years immediately ahead, there were to be a number of occasions in which it appeared that the fierce confrontations of party thwarted rather than promoted the national interest.

. . .

UNDER-SECRETARY FOR THE COLONIES

Campbell-Bannerman had formed his Liberal government in December 1905 and, to the surprise of some in his new party it was as a junior minister that Churchill fought and won his seat. The Prime Minister was well aware that he was taking a risk in offering Winston an appointment. Veteran Liberals regarded the new arrival with suspicion: since he was only too evidently a young man in a hurry, he should be made to wait. It was indeed the case that Churchill had a lot to learn about the Liberal Party. In the 1906 parliament, religious Nonconformists clustered on the Liberal benches in greater numbers than at any time since Cromwell. Militant Dissent was a strange world to Churchill and he showed little wish to enter a Nonconformist chapel, yet it was a vital element in Liberalism at this time. There were good grounds for supposing that Churchill would have no enthusiasm for Temperance legislation. And where did he stand on Irish Home Rule? On this matter the Liberals would supposedly proceed step by step, but even as a Liberal Churchill still declared that he would not support any Irish legislation which might injure the effective integrity of the United Kingdom. And where did he stand on social policy? Back in 1901 he had read Seebohm Rowntree's newly-published *Poverty: A Study of Town Life* – an investigation into social conditions in the city of York. Commenting that he could see little glory in an Empire which could rule the waves but could not flush its own sewers, he looked for a middle-of-the-road policy 'to co-ordinate development and expansion with the progress of social comfort and health'. It was not clear whether his ideas, only loosely-developed though they were, would appeal to Liberals.

In these circumstances it is perhaps not surprising that Churchill decided to accept the post of Under-Secretary for the Colonies. The future settlement of South Africa was high on the agenda and no one could deny that he had first-hand experience of the country. He also realised that he would have scope to make his mark in the Commons since Lord Elgin, the Secretary of State and his superior, sat in the House of Lords. Churchill had held no high opinion of Elgin when the Colonial Secretary had been Viceroy in India and he had been a mere subaltern. In their new relationship, Churchill was itching to assume as much power as he could, but Elgin cannily held on to the reins. It is clear that from the outset Winston relished office and threw himself into its many different aspects with characteristic exuberance. Elgin decided to give Churchill access to all business, without forfeiting his own ultimate control.[7]

The substantive issues initially before the two men concerned South Africa. Churchill successfully urged a new constitution for the Transvaal with a generous franchise (on the mistaken assumption that it would help the 'British' element). He talked eloquently about the need for reconciliation between Briton and Boer, a view which he had come to at the end of his time in South Africa. Everywhere in the world both great empires and small peoples would gain encouragement by such an example. What was and remains difficult is to penetrate behind the rhetoric. He had not abandoned his imperial enthusiasm in becoming a Liberal, but the Liberals were a little embarrassed by empire. He refused to be brow-beaten by zealots, like Leo Amery, into advancing plans for closer coordination. Drawing an analogy with the six-hundred-year construction of Cologne Cathedral, Churchill unusually urged patience – 'Don't let us be in too much of a hurry'. The materials to be used in the construction and consolidation of the British Empire were both more intractable and intangible than those used by masons. To some extent, 'colonials' were being talked down to – and there was never any rush to dine with the Australian Prime Minister, Alfred Deakin, whose proposals seemed disturbingly direct. It was, of course, partly because the air was thick with talk of imperial preference that the tone of the British government was so negative. 'We shall not give one farthing preference on a single peppercorn', declared Churchill. Asquith, the Chancellor of the Exchequer, bluntly told the colonial premiers in 1907 that the British government would not treat 'foreigners' and 'the colonies' differently. In his own address Churchill claimed that when imperial unification had been carried a stage further the conference would stand out in the history of the British Empire as an occasion when one grand wrong turn had been avoided.[8]

It may reasonably be doubted whether imperial unification could ever have been possible – the concept is in any case highly ambiguous – but, since it was not achieved, the grand claims that a wrong turn was avoided in 1907 now seem somewhat hollow. Was the great imperialist really interested in Empire after all? It certainly seemed that there was little desire to understand the self-governing colonies. During his time at the Colonial Office he developed an increasing concern for 'native peoples', though he had no particular regret that the treaty which ended the South African war virtually precluded the possibility of a franchise for 'natives'. The Liberal Empire, as Churchill increasingly conceived it, was an empire founded upon the rule of law. There would be justice for all people subjected to British rule, and he busied himself, in particular cases, in seeking to ensure that this phrase was more than rhetoric. Butchering natives was wrong, and perhaps the 'pacification' of territory such as Northern Nigeria was not so very different. In East Africa, however, which he visited in 1907, there was apparently a much more joyous atmosphere. He could not resist the temptation to write articles about his experiences and a book, *My African Journey*, subsequently emerged. In Uganda, he had no hesitation in consenting, on the spot, to the annexation of yet more territory. He did not for one moment suppose that 'natives' were in any condition to share in the control of the benevolent structure that was being maintained for their benefit. And there was no escaping the fact that the entire enterprise rested upon power.

An increasing ambiguity about empire was not uncharacteristic even of such supposed 'Liberal Imperialists' as Grey, the Foreign Secretary, or Asquith, the Chancellor, but what added to the complexity of Churchill's outlook was a personal enthusiasm for matters military which they certainly did not share.[9] In 1906 he attended German army manoeuvres in Silesia (and presented the Kaiser with a copy of his *Life of Lord Randolph Churchill*), and in 1907 he visited French manoeuvres. The direct connection between his attendance and his ministerial responsibilities was not immediate, but that did not deter him. Since his return to the United Kingdom he had also ventured on to the European mainland for holidays, but he did not seek political contacts of any substance. His military expeditions (and the enthusiastic dressing up in military uniform which accompanied them) aroused suspicion in some Liberal circles that he was a 'militarist' at heart and that his conversion to the party of 'peace, retrenchment and reform' was only superficial. For Churchill, however, military power existed and it was folly to ignore its potential significance.

It was apparent, too, that in other respects Churchill did not hold to a narrow interpretation of his departmental responsibilities. In October 1906, for example, in a major speech in Glasgow he began with some remarks on South Africa, but then broadened into a wide-ranging consideration of 'Liberalism and Socialism'. He used the language of the 'New Liberalism' and stated that the State had increasingly to concern itself with the care of the sick, the aged and children. The attempt to form a Labour Party would split progressive opinion and only benefit the Tories. A line should be drawn below which persons should not be allowed to live and labour, but above which they might rise. Competitive selection was a vital engine yet he argued that the whole tendency of civilisation was towards the multiplication of the collective functions of society.[10] Such speeches were designed to stress the genuine character of his conversion to Liberalism and to draw the attention of his superiors to the fact that his interests were not confined to colonial questions.

Such eloquence did indeed have the desired result. Churchill was an obvious candidate for promotion when Asquith formed his first Cabinet on the resignation of Campbell-Bannerman in April 1908. Various possibilities were canvassed, but in the end Churchill became President of the Board of Trade, occupying the post which Lloyd George had vacated on succeeding Asquith as Chancellor of the Exchequer. He would have a place in the Cabinet – and thus become, at thirty-three, the youngest Cabinet minister for nearly half a century. Ministers were still required to submit themselves for re-election once they accepted office and Churchill experienced the humiliation of defeat in his Manchester constituency, but his career was rescued when he fought and won in Dundee shortly afterwards. Once this obstacle was overcome he was free to be the Cabinet minister he had long aspired to be.

. . .

PRESIDENT OF THE BOARD OF TRADE

A certain disreputableness still hung over him. A few months earlier, in a private letter to the Colonial Secretary, the Permanent Secretary in the Colonial Office described Churchill as 'most tiresome to deal with'. His restless energy, his desire for notoriety and his 'lack of moral perception' gave rise to much concern. He would give trouble – 'as his father did'.[11] Some members of the Opposition continued to find him a 'born cad' and believed that he had no tact or discretion. That was another way of saying that he ought not to be a Cabinet Minister.

A politician makes the leap into the Cabinet with unpredictable consequences. Churchill had reached the inner circle of British power with great speed and at an early age. His new colleagues, men like Grey, the Foreign Secretary or Lloyd George, the Chancellor of the Exchequer, and Asquith, the Prime Minister himself, had all been in parliament for far longer than Churchill and they had little doubt that they were his seniors. On the other hand, although Asquith himself had been Home Secretary in the early 1890s, the Conservative dominance over the next decade inevitably meant that this leading group of ministers and other colleagues had little more direct experience of what it was like to serve in a Cabinet than Churchill himself. It was not in Churchill's nature to be bashful, but in these circumstances he saw no reason even to attempt to defer to the ripe wisdom of his older colleagues. There is reason to suppose that from time to time he feared that he too would die in early middle age. That premonition may in part explain the restless energy which Permanent Secretaries apparently found so alarming.

The Board of Trade did not necessarily seem the most appropriate post for Churchill to occupy. No one could accuse him of having a commercial background. However, much to the dismay of Socialist intelllectuals like Sidney and Beatrice Webb, British government did not proceed on the assumption that ministers had any special personal expertise to contribute to their ministries. A successful Cabinet Minister might be someone about whom his Permanent Secretary wrote critical notes. Few supposed that Winston would wish to end his days at the Board of Trade. Indeed, the ambition of this young 'Napoleon' was so blatant as to be risible. His desire for a place in the front ranks of the Cabinet was so obvious that a Prime Minister would only have supposed that he need worry about more devious characters. In any case, even opponents agreed that the Asquith Cabinet was staffed with able men, all of whom, in their different ways, were eager to make their mark. It would be very strange if they wished to make way for their junior colleague with any degree of urgency.

The obvious task, therefore, was to conduct his own ministry efficiently, but that would not be sufficient in itself. He had to find policies and issues which would make his senior colleagues take note of his efforts. Yet his progress might be hindered if they became impatient with his demands and irritated by his methods. Such a twin strategy may seem self-evidently the best course in retrospect, but we may wonder whether Churchill evaluated his position in quite such a calculated manner. It was a common supposition that he acted intuitively and impulsively. There was, however, a new development which might just possibly modify his behaviour; in the year in which he became a Cabinet Minister he married Clementine Hozier, an attractive girl, ten years younger than himself, who, somewhat to Winston's surprise, seemed to possess 'much intellectual quality' and strong reserves of 'noble sentiment'. It was to be a marriage which would endure, but she could have had little notion that Winston's way of life and sense of priorities would change to any significant degree. He saw no reason to apologize for talking politics to Lloyd George in the vestry of St Margaret's, Westminster, after the wedding ceremony. It was the summer recess, after all, and there was a lot to catch up on.

The Cabinet had been invited to the ceremony and there was general interest in the event. It was unusual to have a Cabinet Minister marrying for the first time, and Churchill was probably the first one to arrive at his wedding in an electric brougham. However, many colleagues happened to be in distant parts of the world, such as Scotland, and chose not to return. It was evident, nevertheless, that there was personal goodwill towards Churchill, even after a few months of shared government. These personal relations were important because Winston still remained something of an oddity amongst his colleagues. He was not a lawyer, he was not a university man and he was the only ex-soldier.

It is not difficult to see why it was with Lloyd George that he appeared to strike his firmest initial alliance. At first sight, since the contrast in their social backgrounds was greater than between any two other members of the Cabinet it might have been expected to make intimacy difficult. Yet both men had reached their high positions by unusual routes and recognised in each other a certain indifference to the codes and conventions which appeared still to prevail in the solid English middle classes to which neither of them belonged. Both men had a necessary interest in the acquisition of money (or goods), without which their pursuit of power would be impossible. Churchill accepted without difficulty the generous offer of the Jewish banker, Sir Ernest Cassel, to furnish the sitting room in his new house, and enjoyed holidays given him by Baron de Forest. He laid himself open to the suspicion that neither generous friend acted without some expectation of future favour. A few years later, in the Marconi scandal, Lloyd George's conduct came close to destroying his own career and bringing down the Liberal government. Churchill could never bring himself to share Lloyd George's enthusiasm for golf, or to understand the Chancellor's periodic preference for a simple cut of mutton, but they shared more than one cigar together while they reflected on how best to tackle 'the social problem'.

In March 1908, in the Liberal weekly *The Nation*, Churchill called social reform 'the untrodden field of politics'. The Liberal Party had championed personal freedom, but it had become acutely conscious that unless there was a measure of social and economic independence political freedom was incomplete. He began to talk about 'organisation' of industry and a 'scientific' treatment of the problems of the poor and unemployed. Here was language redolent of the Webbs (whom he met) and of those Liberal writers who believed that they were sketching out a philosophically coherent 'New Liberalism'. However, Churchill had no interest in abstract speculation about the nature of the State. He took what to him appeared a common sense view. Intervention was not 'right' or 'wrong' in itself – everything depended upon particular circumstances. With a wisdom that was not inconvenient, he suspected that 'the truth' lay between 'individualism' and 'collectivism'. He shared with Lloyd George an ability to sense the sort of political discourse which the times appeared to need and an interest in contributing pungent phrases to the public debate rather than lengthy expositions to academic discussion.[12]

Tory critics were not slow to find this 'New Churchill' even less convincing than the old, though in drawing attention to the disparity between Churchill's continuing personal lifestyle and his crusade for the 'left-out millions' they invited the turning back of such criticism on themselves. Churchill himself could see no substance in the accusations of hypocrisy brought against him. It was true that he liked champagne; that he never travelled third-class; that he never packed his own travel bag. In these and other respects he certainly belonged to the 'vanguard' which enjoyed 'all the delights of all the ages', but he never supposed that a life of comfort precluded a real concern for the 'rearguard'. 'Equality' was neither obtainable nor desirable, but there should be 'levelling up'. Someone with a sybaritic disposition did not need to assume an ascetic demeanour to achieve this objective.

Churchill convinced himself of this without undue difficulty and set about his tasks with a zeal that was already legendary.

During these years Winston was chiefly associated with two areas of policy: 'sweated labour' (to be remedied by creating Trade Boards), and unemployment (to be mitigated by a system of labour exchanges and unemployment insurance).[13] The two latter proposals were firmly linked together in Churchill's mind, but the financial complexities inherent in an insurance scheme meant that he had to be content with the creation of the Labour Exchanges. It fell to Lloyd George to introduce a National Insurance scheme a little later. Churchill's efforts were important, but it would be a distortion of perspective to see them as either the centrepieces of the government's programme or the initial steps in an envisaged 'Welfare State'. Even so, Churchill brought a passion to these matters and an irrepressible ability to be feeling his way to what he called 'a considerable policy'. He felt confident that the country cared more about these social issues than about mere political change. The Liberals could surely develop a tremendous policy in 'Social Organisation' and he had no problem in urging a 'big slice of Bismarckianism' (that is to say the social welfare measures introduced by Bismarck in Germany). Such was his enthusiasm that it did not seem to occur to him that a Prime Minister might not altogether relish lengthy communications on these matters dated 26 and 29 December (1908). It seems that after digesting his big slice of Christmas pudding, served at Blenheim by powdered footmen, Churchill had nothing better to do on Boxing Day than switch back to politics. One of the Prime Minister's succinct replies, which confessed that he had not fully mastered Churchill's ideas on afforestation, could be taken to indicate a certain weariness and wariness on his part.

It also became clear that Churchill still found it impossible to confine his thoughts to his own departmental concerns. Of course, it could be said that the 1909 budget, with its proposed tax increases, and the ensuing battle with the House of Lords to achieve its passage, came very close to those concerns. Certainly, Churchill threw himself into the struggle as though he were directing it. A Budget League was speedily formed and he became its chairman. It was the League which organised the famous Limehouse meeting at which Lloyd George excoriated large landowners. The two men were in close contact through the summer and Churchill's pedigree ensured that his unrestrained verbal assault on the titled landed class was held to constitute a particular kind of betrayal of his own kind. His speeches at Edinburgh and Leicester caused consternation. His reference in the latter to a miserable minority of titled persons who represented nobody troubled the King. His eagerness to take on the Lords troubled the Prime Minister.

There were even times when he troubled himself. His very own family duke was not pleased. Even so, he pressed on – yet he could not quite banish the suspicion that he was more two-faced than was acceptably normal in a leading politician. Opposition gossip, which could not take his lambasting at face value, suggested that Churchill, disappointed to be outstripped in radicalism by Lloyd George, was contemplating withdrawing altogether from the sphere of party politics. In fact, he seemed more committed than ever and in the final months of 1909 embarked on speeches up and down the country which earned the apprehensive admiration of the Prime Minister. His collected thoughts on *The People's Rights* appeared just in time for the first General Election in 1910.

In September 1909 he gave the peers a mild rest and took himself off to Germany to attend German army manoeuvres once more. He had a few words with the Kaiser, who referred to him by his first name. He also made a pilgrimage to the battlefield at Blenheim and a Labour Exchange in Strasbourg. As always, he observed his surroundings carefully. He did not care for the Tiepolo ceilings in the old palace at Würzburg where he dined in great splendour; they belonged to the 'whipped cream & sponge cake style of painting'. He imagined Napoleon dining in state on such an occasion in Germany about a century earlier. He had a sense of the tragedies of European history, not shared with the same imagination by any of his Cabinet colleagues, as he watched the distinguished company in the flickering light of a thousand candles. This was not Bangalore or Omdurman or Johannesburg; it was the heart of old Europe and perhaps the struggle for its mastery was not over yet. The scene evoked two contrary reactions. He could not deny that he felt the enormous fascination of war but he also felt ever more strongly 'what vile & wicked folly & barbarism it all is'. What conclusions about power were to be drawn from his observations of that 'terrible engine' which was the German army? A President of the Board of Trade did not normally worry about such things, but he was not a normal President of the Board of Trade.

He had come to these matters in Cabinet with inherited prejudices. He quickly presented his seniors with detailed proposals for army reform which astounded Haldane, the Secretary of State for War. They embellished Winston's long-held conviction that the British Army was not an instrument to fight in Europe and it was not wise to spend additional money to pretend that it could do so. Haldane just about held off the challenge, but Churchill's exposition had impressed. Winston also took part in the battle in the Cabinet in early 1909 over naval expenditure before agreeing to the compromise which authorised the construction of six Dreadnoughts. He did so on the comprehensive scale that his colleagues were coming to expect. Churchill's opposition to increased expenditure stemmed from two sources: fear that it would jeopardise his social reform proposals and disbelief in the supposed threat. An exasperated Prime Minister threatened at one point to 'cashier' both Churchill and Lloyd George. The Foreign Secretary expressed his displeasure at the fact that Churchill was speaking on foreign policy in his constituency and elsewhere, particularly when he made claims – as in August 1908 – that Britain and Germany had nothing to fight about, had no prize to fight for and no place to fight in.

A year later, he still seemed to have the same view but, even so, Germany worried him. Unlike Sir Edward Grey, who did not allow his mind or feelings to be infected by actual experience of European countries, Churchill's perceptions of power relationships were shaped, or at least guided, by direct experience. He had been talking for months about the need to 'Germanise' important aspects of British social organisation but he now sensed the extent to which change could not be grafted on from outside. More generally, the Germans struck him as alarmingly efficient, but somehow they did not possess the invaluable British instinct. The British moved more slowly but took bigger steps. He was struck by the complete divorce in German life between the Imperialists and Socialists. He suspected that a period of severe internal strain was approaching in Germany. He had to admit that the German government might seek relief from it by external adventure. He came back home reinforced in his conviction that the Liberal Party could prevent the social polarisation he saw in Germany if it struck boldly for serious change within a social order which could avoid the disaster of Socialism. The vehemence of his language reflected his anxiety that he had little time in which to preserve a country to which he became more devoted the more he travelled abroad.

. . .

HOME SECRETARY

It was not only abroad that he travelled. He was one of the most active Liberal platform speakers in the General Election campaigns of January 1910. Even the Prime Minister felt that his support would be valuable in his campaign in East Fife. Churchill expected a reward when Asquith came to form his new administration and was offered the Irish Office. He declined this offer and indicated that he would only be satisfied with either the Admiralty or the Home Office. The Prime Minister offered the latter post. Churchill, at the age of thirty-five, became the youngest Home Secretary since Sir Robert Peel in 1822.

The seniority of the post was unquestioned, symbolised by the fact that it was his duty each day during the Parliamentary session to write to the King concerning the business of the Commons. In practice, his duties extended from the supervision of arcane aspects of immigration regulation to a central responsibility for the maintenance of law and order. He also had to advise the King on the exercise of his prerogative of mercy. Specifically, there were weighty problems of prison administration which required immediate attention. Churchill's instincts remained liberal, perhaps because he had the unique experience among Home Secretaries of having been in prison himself. Amongst other changes, he introduced more time to pay fines, reduced the amount of solitary confinement and took steps to improve the after-care of prisoners. As a result, he found it not inappropriate that he was generally regarded as a 'reforming' Home Secretary.

The divergent pressures of his office were exemplified in his dealings with the coal industry. On the one hand, he could rightly claim credit for the 1911 Mines Act which improved the safety regulations for pits, though the measure was actually passed after he left the Home Office. On the other hand, his handling of the miners' strike in South Wales in November 1910 brought him criticism which was never entirely to leave him, even at the end of his career. After rioting in the Rhondda Valley, he despatched reinforcements from the Metropolitan Police. Troops were also on stand-by but their role was limited. This did not prevent the view gaining currency that Churchill had been responsible for the provocative deployment of troops. The details of the affair are complex. Churchill's insistence that he was prepared to employ the military upset Labour spokesmen. He was also attacked from some Tory quarters for exercising too much restraint when confronted by serious rioting. The troops were not in fact used, but the events in Tonypandy were to be used by the Left for many decades to come as an illustration of Churchill's 'aggressiveness'.

The summer of 1911 saw the repetition of many of these problems as industrial disputes worsened. A series of transport strikes culminated in a national railway strike. It was easy to believe that these strikes were coordinated. There was much talk of 'Syndicalism' and of famine. A revolution was believed to be imminent on Merseyside. Churchill's response was initially measured but in the sultry month of August he seems to have become very alarmed. He took the grave step on 19 August of suspending the Army Regulation which required a requisition for troops from a civil authority. Churchill's energetic preparations were bitterly criticised by Labour spokesmen who accused him of behaving as if he were living in a medieval state. In the event, the railway strike was settled within a matter of days and there were no major losses of life. However, the outcome could easily have been different and made Churchill vulnerable to the charge of excessive and provocative zeal. At the beginning of 1911 he had been in the headlines because of his personal intervention in the 'Siege of Sidney Street', as the press called it – the battle against a group of Latvian anarchists. He claimed that it was his duty to see at first hand the sequence of events, but he could be accused of acting in an undignified and theatrical fashion. In the case of the industrial disputes it led to the unfounded accusation that he was 'longing for blood'.

47

There is no doubt, however, that Churchill felt his responsibility for the maintenance of law and order acutely. It has often been suggested that his attitude during this period is testimony to the fact that 'His radicalism had more or less blown itself out and he was beginning to drift towards the right, in many respects his natural home.'[14] It is admitted, however, that his reactions were not unexpected in a Home Secretary. Churchill would have rejected the notion that the upholding of law and order was a sign that he was losing sympathy for the underlying causes of discontent. Orderly change was one thing, violence teetering on the brink of revolution was another. If the State lost control then anarchy threatened. However, the crisis did reveal the precarious position of the government as a whole as it sought to portray itself both as the party of reform and the party of order. Indeed, although Charles Masterman and David Lloyd George, two Liberal colleagues, made critical remarks about Churchill in private, contrasting his stance with their 'conciliatory' attitude, it is arguable that it was the fusion of both approaches which, together with the international crisis which was also occurring in the summer of 1911, made for a successful outcome from the standpoint of the Liberal government. The Cabinet could not have afforded a 'negotiating' Home Secretary at this juncture, however much it was subsequently easy to criticise Churchill's apparent impetuosity, particularly in his dispositions of the military. Winston himself seemed quite unrepentant. He had an acute sense that each office had its particular task within government. His pugnacity was the other side of his determination not to be bullied by groups in society who seemed to him to go beyond the limits of acceptable pressure. He was not unsympathetic to the aspirations of trade unionists or suffragettes but he would not allow them to dictate the appropriate response to their grievances. He could scarcely avoid an 'insider's' understanding of the power of the State. In fact, Asquith understood both that he had served the government's collective purpose admirably and that, as the immediate industrial crisis lessened, it would be politic to move Winston elsewhere.

·   ·   ·

FIRST LORD OF THE ADMIRALTY

It was in September 1911 that Asquith asked Churchill whether he would like to go to the Admiralty. 'Of course', Churchill replied. Haldane had the same desire, but Winston pressed his claim. A reshuffle at this juncture suited the Prime Minister both negatively and positively. It enabled him to please critics of Churchill's performance at the Home Office and also to cause a certain consternation among the admirals. Events during the summer suggested that they needed some disturbance. Even so, the switch was somewhat risky, because he must have realised that Churchill's views about the Royal Navy were in the process of undergoing a sea-change, with somewhat unpredictable consequences. However, although Asquith may have supposed that Churchill thought with his mouth, the words that emerged were undeniably interesting.

Hitherto, Winston had combined a firm belief in 'a supreme and unchallengeable Navy' with the desire for economy which had led him in 1908/9 to campaign with Lloyd George in favour of laying down no more than four Dreadnoughts. He had argued at that time against McKenna, with whom he was now swopping jobs. In the early months of 1911 he was still considered to be in the 'economist' lobby with the Chancellor. In May, with his usual generous interpretation of his duties, he was advising the King that conciliatory remarks about Germany would be welcomed by the 'Peace party' in the country, amongst whom he clearly counted himself.

In July 1911, however, he was roused by the German action in sending a gunboat, *Panther*, to the Moroccan port of Agadir as an indication of German dissatisfaction with the way in which Britain, France and Spain were disregarding German colonial interests. The outcome might have been a settlement from which Britain, in turn, might have been excluded and which would have undermined the *entente* with France which Grey had sustained ever since coming into office. The Foreign Secretary found slightly unexpected support from Lloyd George whose speech at the Mansion House roundly stated that it would be an intolerable humiliation for Britain to be treated as if she were of no account in the Cabinet of nations.

This declaration was largely meant for Berlin, though it had relevance in Paris also.

Churchill reacted with comparable vehemence, telling his wife that Germany would be jolly well mistaken if she thought Morocco could be divided up without John Bull. In an undated memorandum he wrote that if Germany made war on France Britain should join with France. The Germans should be made aware of this likelihood. The crisis coincided with the industrial disputes – Lloyd George used the serious international situation as a reason for a settlement – but despite Churchill's deep involvement in them his interest in international affairs would appear to be even greater. He and Lloyd George were determined to keep Grey 'all progged up' and Winston even went swimming with the Foreign Secretary in order to keep him up to the mark. The relationship with Sir Edward had been strengthening for some time. Grey became his baby son's godfather.[15] Churchill circulated a lengthy memorandum to his colleagues ahead of a crucial meeting of the Committee of Imperial Defence (C.I.D.), to which he was bidden, to be held on 23 August. He envisaged the possibility of a major European struggle in which the decisive encounter would be between Germany and France. Churchill suggested ways in which British influence could be brought to bear and produced an imaginative timetable for the despatch of troops. He exchanged letters eagerly with Lloyd George and for a time both men appeared to think that war was imminent. As far as Churchill was concerned, it would not be a war for Morocco or for Belgium but a war to prevent France from being trampled down by the Prussian junkers.

The Moroccan crisis passed, but the mood in which Churchill approached his new responsibilities was quite different from what it would have been six months earlier. Some of his colleagues were alarmed by the ease with which it was apparently being assumed that British forces would be fighting in France. They were under the impression that no commitment had been made. They were very alarmed by the new 'rampageous strategists' whose activities would upset the balance of the Cabinet. They reminded themselves that Churchill was a military man and that he seemed unduly excited by the prospect of war. His apparent *volte face* on yet another important issue led to further accusations of 'instability'. Churchill was certainly excited. His new post was 'the big thing' and he would pour everything he had into it. He maintained, too, that there was no inconsistency in his views. He had always believed in naval supremacy. What precisely that entailed always had to be a matter of judgment in relation to circumstances. He was not a 'pacifist' – a word just coming into use – and, like any intelligent man, he shifted his ground as those circumstances changed.

His pattern of behaviour on assuming a new office was by now entirely predictable.[16] He was an enthusiast. He wanted to know everything about his new responsibilities and to know it immediately. He prodded and probed every aspect of the navy with a cheerful indifference to *amour-propre*. He was very conscious that he was answerable for the security of the Empire. The stewardship of the greatest navy in the world was in his hands and he would brook no opposition in his determination to master its requirements. Here at last the man and the moment met. In one sense, he was the most powerful man in the country. He could not fail to respond to the drama of his position and he revelled in the myriad naval customs (and uniforms) to which he was now given access. He was the living embodiment of a great tradition. There were innumerable ships which he could be piped aboard. He thrilled at the prospect of living in Admiralty House and seemed oblivious to the problem of paying for the dozen servants who would be needed to make life tolerable there. His wife was somewhat less oblivious.

There could have been no one amongst his colleagues who combined more vividly a delight in the past with a grasp of the present. He delighted in the practical rather than the abstract. A passion for continuity was combined with a zest for modernity: a combination which made it increasingly difficult to fit him into any stereotype. He already had an enthusiasm for motor-cars and was particularly proud to have driven down from Scotland to take up his appointment at the Admiralty in a £610 red Napier which had been delivered to him at Balmoral. His military past gave him every confidence in talking about guns. He paid a visit to a submarine at an early opportunity and seemed genuinely to want to know how it worked. He was anxious to know as much as possible about aeroplanes and, to the alarm of his wife, took to the air in person on numerous occasions. He could justly claim to know the problems and the joys of flying and, as he put it, was in a position 'to understand all the questions of policy wh. will arise in the near future'. His staff and associates came quickly to realise that the First Lord could not be fobbed off with generalities once he was determined to find out the truth.

Such commitment was both welcome and unwelcome amongst the admirals with whom he had to deal. His detailed involvement was both encouraging and annoying. There were to be many times when officers felt that he had gone too far in his criticisms and comments during the course of a visitation. Yet anger was frequently banished as it became clear that his concern was transparently for the welfare of the navy as a whole. He interested himself in rates of pay and took steps to reform an antiquated code of discipline. Here there was continuity with the attitude maintained in his previous posts.

Such popularity as this concern brought him availed little at the highest level. Churchill knew from the outset that he would have a difficult time with the admirals and was determined to live up to expectations. The CID meeting on 23 August, which had precipitated his appointment, had disclosed an inability (stemming from a lack of desire), if the need arose, to transport six divisions to France. A Naval War Staff seemed imperative, but met with opposition from the elderly First Sea Lord, Sir Arthur Wilson. Churchill decided that Wilson had to go, but the question of his replacement led him immediately into issues of power and responsibility. He was determined to have a Naval War Staff and, in three divisions, it was in operation under the First Sea Lord by early 1912. There was, however, a broader question. How far should a civilian minister go in asserting his authority? Churchill made it clear that he would not delegate to the admirals as much power of decision in the Board of Admiralty as they had been accustomed to having. Needless to say, Churchill did not approach these issues with a virgin mind. Over the previous few years he had struck up a remarkable friendship with the mercurial figure of Sir John Fisher from whom he had already gleaned many insights into the problems of the Royal Navy. It was tempting to think of bringing him back to replace Wilson but Churchill recognised that Fisher was not a man to play second fiddle. In addition, the appointment of Fisher would only reopen personal wounds and renewed feuding with his opponents. Churchill decided upon Sir Francis Bridgeman as First Sea Lord and Prince Louis of Battenberg as Second Sea Lord with a view to the succession, a succession which he insisted upon after only a year. These and other decisions produced an ever-growing list of disgruntled admirals. Insofar as there was a common criticism, it rested in the fact that Churchill appeared to make up his mind about people so quickly and without adequate investigation.

The First Lord's ruthless reshuffling of the naval pack was his most conspicuous exercise of power in his career so far. His boldness would rebound against him if he failed to convince both his colleagues and the public at large that the navy was secure. He certainly threw off his earlier opposition to naval expenditure. It seemed that when he changed his mind he did so in spectacular leaps rather than in unobtrusive shifts. 'The whole character of the German fleet', he told the CID on 11 July 1912, 'shows that it is designed for aggressive and offensive action of the largest possible character in the North Sea or the North Atlantic . . .'. In public, at Glasgow and elsewhere he emphasised that the British Navy was a necessity: the German Navy was not. It was a theme which was constantly reiterated, though he also unsuccessfully floated the idea of a 'naval holiday'. Inevitably, naval policy interacted with foreign policy, and in general Churchill was in agreement with the broad lines being pursued by Grey. He was well aware in 1912–13 of the implications of the disposition of British forces as between the Mediterranean and the North Sea. Like the Foreign Secretary over the entire range of policy, Churchill strove to find an arrangement whereby the British and French navies would cooperate in the event of war: there was no undertaking that Britain would automatically intervene. However, he too was storing up certain 'obligations of honour' for the future.

These were broad strategic issues but the war might be won or lost on details. Precisely because he immersed himself in them to an unusual degree his record has attracted particular praise and criticism. At a general level, he may be said to have injected a degree of urgency which was previously missing. Specifically, he could claim the credit for the development of the fast fifteen-inch-gunned battleships which were to prove vital. He was also quick to perceive the need to change over from coal- to oil-fired battleships and, through the Anglo-Persian Oil Company, to ensure a source of supply. On the debit side, shortcomings in British shells, torpedoes and gunnery in general can in part be attributed to his desire to see production at the expense of testing. The Naval War Staff had scarcely bedded down before war came – but that was not Churchill's fault.

In general, it was a record of which he could be proud by 1914 – if his premiss of likely war is conceded. It was the case, however, that a substantial section of the Liberal Party was unwilling to accept this likelihood. Throughout, Churchill was not only battling against various elements in the navy, but he was also working against the grain of his party. This was particularly apparent in the struggles surrounding the last two Naval Estimates before the war. This time he was in conflict with Lloyd George in particular – but the Chancellor appeared to epitomise the mood of the hour and Churchill had to give a little ground.

There was no doubt that the First Lord had shown great energy and industry. There had, however, been some compensations, though these in turn earned him criticism. The Admiralty yacht, the *Enchantress*, proved to have other uses than merely to take the First Lord from one naval base to another. It proved possible not only to call on Lloyd George at Criccieth but to cruise in the Mediterranean. *Punch* noted these jaunts without much ferocity but the *National Review*, guardian of economy, wanted to know how much coal had been consumed, how many lobsters had been eaten and how many magnums of champagne had been consumed. Churchill did not arrange for the information to be supplied.

Moments of conspicuous relaxation apart, Churchill's devotion to the navy inevitably occasioned some criticism. 'He is too concentrated on his particular office', wrote the newspaper proprietor Lord Riddell in his diary in December 1912.[17] In fact, although the navy occupied most of his time, it would not have been in character to exclude all other matters from his attention. It would have been surprising if his father's son would have been allowed to forget Ireland. In his early years as a Liberal MP, when 'step by step' rather than a comprehensive Irish measure had been general Liberal policy, his reservations about Home Rule had not stood out. Between 1908 and 1910 he appeared to express more sym-

pathy for Irish self-government, so long as the supremacy of
the Imperial Parliament was not jeopardised. He seemed to
be encouraged by the example of the South African settlement
to believe that a satisfactory *modus vivendi* between Britain and
Ireland could be reached. He also had his eye on Irish-
descended voters in the constituencies he sought to represent.

The 1910 General Elections placed the Irish Nationalists in
a strong position to exert influence in the Commons. The
Liberal Party was now under pressure to move specifically
towards a measure of Irish Home Rule. Churchill did not
stand aloof from the issue, as prudence might have dictated.
Not only did he privately instruct himself on Irish history,
but his interest in achieving a 'reconciliation' was known on
the Irish side. 'All of us count on *you* to put Home Rule
through', wrote the Irish leader, John Redmond, to Churchill
in February 1911. However, his first move was to attempt an
oblique approach to the problem. In the following months he
canvassed the Cabinet with various proposals for 'Devolution'
within the United Kingdom as a whole. If they had found
favour, the Irish issue would have ceased to be a 'special
case'. The ideas were imaginative, though not without problems, but since they had little apparent appeal he dropped
them. It was Churchill who in early August announced in the
Commons that the government intended to bring forward a
Home Rule measure. In a speech in his constituency a couple
of months later, he confirmed his own commitment and spoke
scathingly of 'Ulster will fight, Ulster will be right!' as a
slogan from which every 'street bully' and 'crazy fanatic'
could draw consolation.

There matters stood when he transferred to the Admiralty.
He could have left Ireland alone, but he would not. He agreed
to speak in Belfast on 8 February 1912.[18] The meeting was
originally to have been held in the Ulster Hall, where his
father had spoken in 1886, but eventually was held in a leaky
marquee with heavy rain falling. Feelings ran high in the city
and troops were standing by. Churchill was open to the
obvious criticism that he was a 'renegade' while for his part
he denounced Carson, the Ulster Unionist leader, and Bonar
Law, the Leader of the Opposition, for their encouragement
of 'bigotry' and 'lawlessness'. Churchill tried to twist his
father's words into a new slogan, 'Let Ulster fight for the
dignity and honour of Ireland', but he made no serious

CHURCHILL

attempt to understand the anxieties of Protestant Unionists. Even if in fact Lord Randolph's own position in 1886 was more subtle than Unionist legend would have it, Winston's visit could only have appeared provocative. The Irish Home Rule Bill was introduced in April 1912. Speaking in the Commons, Churchill accused Bonar Law of 'almost treasonable activity' in his opposition. In July Bonar Law deliberately chose a Unionist rally at Blenheim to declare that he could not imagine any length of resistance to which Ulster could go in which he would not be prepared to give them his support. By the autumn, Churchill had come to the view that 'three or four counties' could be offered the option of remaining at Westminster for five or ten years. The important thing was to get the Irish Parliament set up. Orange misgivings would then be overcome 'in the course of a few years'. For different reasons, neither the Opposition nor the Irish Nationalists would support such an outcome – at least not at this point.

A year later, when the Home Rule Bill had passed twice through the Commons, and had been rejected twice by the Lords, and the prospect of civil war in Ireland, a war which might also spread to Britain, had become imminent, Churchill returned to the search for a solution. Between September and November 1913 it is not an exaggeration to describe Churchill as the most active member of the Cabinet in this regard. It suited many of his colleagues, including the Prime Minister, to let him make most of the running. In public he distinguished between an Ulster Unionist claim for special treatment and a claim to block the path of the rest of Ireland. It was Churchill again in conversation and correspondence with Bonar Law, Austen Chamberlain and F.E. Smith who sought to explore how to make that distinction in a practical scheme. Nationalists suspected that he was tacitly accepting that there were 'two nations' in Ireland. By early March 1914 the Cabinet proposed a compromise – which did not enjoy Opposition support – whereby Ulster counties could vote themselves out of Home Rule for a period of six years.

In the light of this concession, Churchill now reverted to a firm line. He told a Bradford audience on 14 March that if the concession were spurned then it was time to 'put these grave matters to the proof'. At long last, there was some correlation between his own departmental responsibilities and

56

the Irish question: Churchill ordered a battleship squadron to take up station off the Isle of Arran with a view to sending landing parties into Ulster. The 'mutiny' at the Curragh, outside Dublin, a week later, coupled with gun-running to Ulster, pointed to a tragic and violent outcome. Asquith countermanded the movement of the battleships: he subsequently, but probably falsely, claimed that he had not known of the original order. Opposition spokesmen accused Churchill of trying to goad the Ulster Volunteers so that he could launch an 'Ulster pogrom'. Carson depicted him as the 'Belfast butcher'.

Churchill defended himself in strong terms. He was adamant that if a rebellion came, it would be put down and if civil war came, the government would do its best to conquer. However, taking what he called the 'biggest risk' of his career, he made a final appeal (it seems on his own initiative) to Carson to accept the proposed Amendment to the Home Rule Bill. In return, Churchill would use his best efforts to make Ireland 'an integrative unit in a federal system'. Churchill claimed that this offer 'transformed the political situation' and indeed, in July, an all-party conference took place at Buckingham Palace in order to find a solution. It failed. The Cabinet met on 24 July to press ahead with its amendments. However, the problems of Ulster and Ireland were overtaken. The Foreign Secretary reported the Austrian ultimatum to Serbia and the prospect that the four continental Great Powers would be drawn into a war. The First Lord of the Admiralty had a good deal to worry about.

· · ·

NOTES AND REFERENCES

1. Randolph S. Churchill, *Winston S. Churchill*, Volume I, Companion Part II, p. 765.
2. *Ibid.* pp. 322–3.
3. *Ibid.* pp. 518–9.
4. Arthur Mejia, 'Lord Hugh Cecil: Religion and Liberty' in J.A. Thompson and Arthur Mejia, eds., *Edwardian Conservatism: Five Studies in Adaptation*, London, 1988, p. 21.
5. John Vincent, ed., *The Crawford Papers: The Journals of David Lindsay, twenty-seventh Earl of Crawford and tenth Earl*

of Balcarres 1871–1940 during the years 1891 to 1940, Manchester, 1984, pp. 59 and 83.

6. Winston S. Churchill, *Lord Randolph Churchill*, Vol. II, London, 1906, pp.488–9.

7. Ronald Hyam, *Elgin and Churchill at the Colonial Office 1905–1908: The Watershed of the Empire-Commonwealth*, London, 1968.

8. *Ibid.* p. 342.

9. M. Beloff, *Imperial Sunset: Volume 1: Britain's Liberal Empire, 1897–1921*, London, 1969, pp. 112–16: H.C.G. Matthew, *The Liberal Imperialists: The Ideas and Politics of a Post-Gladstonian Elite*, Oxford, 1973, pp. 150–223.

10. Winston S. Churchill, *Liberalism and the Social Problem*, London, 1909, pp.67–84. In general on Churchill's attitudes see P. Addison, 'Winston Churchill and the Working Class, 1900–1914' in J.M. Winter, ed., *The Working Class in Modern British History: Essays in Honour of Henry Pelling*, Cambridge, 1983, pp. 43–64.

11. Hyam, *Elgin and Churchill*, p. 502.

12. P. Clarke, *Liberals and Social Democrats*, Cambridge, 1978, p. 117.

13. R. Davidson, *Whitehall and the Labour Problem in late-Victorian and Edwardian Britain*, London, 1985.

14. Piers Brendon, *Winston Churchill: A Brief Life*, London, 1984, pp. 56–7.

15. Keith Robbins, *Sir Edward Grey*, London, 1971, p. 244.

16. Richard Hough, *Former Naval Person: Churchill and the Wars at Sea*, London, 1985; Stephen Roskill, *Churchill and the Admirals*, London, 1977; Bernard Semmel, *Liberalism & Naval Strategy: Ideology, Interest and Sea Power during the Pax Britannica*, Boston, 1986, pp.131–7.

17. Randolph S. Churchill, *Winston S. Churchill*, Volume II, *The Young Statesman 1901–1914*, London, 1967, p. 607.

18. *Ibid.* pp. 461–8.

Chapter 3

MAKING WAR AND PEACE
1914–1922

FIRST LORD OF THE ADMIRALTY 1914–15

The casual observer of British naval manoeuvres in July 1914 would have been persuaded that Britain was a very great power. King George V inspected the combined fleets of the Royal Navy assembled at Spithead. It took more than six hours for this armada to pass before the Royal Yacht. Churchill described the sight as 'the greatest assemblage of naval power ever witnessed in the history of the world'.[1] The responsibility for its effective deployment was his – and one immediate problem pressed. The mobilisation had been agreed by the Cabinet in the spring and was not directly occasioned by European developments. Should it be allowed to disperse? It does not appear that the matter was discussed at the Cabinet on 24 July. Churchill left for a Norfolk beach where he played with his children and spoke spasmodically with the First Sea Lord over a poor telephone line. Even though Churchill returned to London late on 26 July, Prince Louis believed, at least subsequently, that his political master had left him to take the crucial decision to 'stand the Fleet fast'.

Like some other Cabinet colleagues at this juncture, Winston found the march of events sinister, but still could not quite believe that they would lead inexorably to war. His office gave him a pivotal position, but he knew equally that he did not have the power to take the country to war. It was unclear in what precise circumstances Britain would intervene and whether the Cabinet would hold together in reaching such a decision. Churchill did not appear to suffer from the anxieties and inhibitions which afflicted some of his colleagues. He described himself to his wife as being 'interested, geared up and happy', though he recognised that it was horrible 'to be built like that'. He confessed that the energetic preparations in which he was engaged had a 'hideous fascination' for him. Yet he still wanted to do his best for peace, as he put it, and would not wrongfully strike the blow.[2] He was perhaps the happiest man in the Cabinet, or perhaps the only happy man. His task, as he saw it, was to do all he could in these critical days to place the Navy on a war footing. However, there remained prominent colleagues who believed that energetic steps, for example, the despatch of the First Fleet into the North Sea, would appear provocative and precipitate the conflict they still wished to avoid. Churchill circumvented the Cabinet in this particular by obtaining a reluctant private grunt of assent from the Prime Minister. As always, Churchill's vigour impressed Asquith but the Prime Minister's own preoccupation at this stage was with Cabinet unity. Churchill did his best to persuade Lloyd George, supposedly a waverer, that British intervention would be necessary. In other quarters in the Liberal Party, however, the First Lord's manifest enthusiasm was counter-productive. His eagerness to talk to leading Unionists was a sign that he was prepared for a Coalition government to take Britain to war if the Liberals split. In the event, however, the German violation of Belgian neutrality reduced the number of resignations and it was a Liberal Cabinet which took Britain to war. 'Commence hostilities against Germany' was the message flashed by Churchill at 11pm on 4 August 1914.

At this precise moment, it was a sense of exhilaration and excitement which predominated. There was a widespread public expectation that there would be an early and decisive battle in the North Sea which could bring the war to an early conclusion. Churchill himself seems to have been less certain. In fact, he ordered the navy, just after the outbreak of the war, to plan on the basis of a war lasting one year, with most effort in the first six months.

He had expressed himself earlier on the subject of war on a number of occasions. He had prophesied, for instance, as early as 1901 that a European war would be very different from the colonial wars, even from the South African war, to which the British people had become accustomed. It might last for several years and engage the entire resources of the State. At the end, there might be little to choose between the ruin of the vanquished and the exhaustion of the conqueror. In addition, he suspected that 'the democracy' would be more vindictive than Cabinets. The wars of peoples would be more terrible than the wars of kings. His experience of government over the ensuing dozen years had deepened his understanding of what mobilisation might entail. His knowledge of 'the democracy', too, had deepened. Some dissident Liberals and Socialists had quickly formed a Union of Democratic Control. They were committed to the proposition that 'the people' never wanted wars and were only drawn into them as a result of the machinations of their rulers. Churchill knew very well how reluctant many of his colleagues had been to fight and also saw for himself some of the signs of popular enthusiasm which had perhaps helped to persuade them of its necessity. Yet he also knew that 'the democracy' was fickle. Who could tell where power would really lie as the scale of war unfolded?

Immediately, the problems of power were localised but still serious. The government was still Liberal and Churchill had no particular reason to be apprehensive about his colleagues. Yet Cabinet government in wartime would inevitably prove a difficult business. Could 'collective responsibility' function? Would the existing modes of discussion and decision-taking suffice? Formal power rested with the Prime Minister, but was Asquith a 'war leader'? If it became obvious that he was not, who might succeed him and how could such a transfer of power be engineered? It was possible, too, that sooner or later 'national unity' would require the formation of a Coalition government. In such circumstances, Churchill could find himself in political difficulties. Whether and when there might be a General Election, or on what terms the government's life might be extended beyond its legal limit, added to uncertainty. Churchill's political base, in short, was reasonably secure, but not beyond challenge, given these imponderables.

It was in his own departmental sphere, however, that issues of power and responsibility pressed most acutely. British tradition and convention asserted civilian political supremacy in military departments, but there was not, and perhaps could not be, precise guidance on the respective spheres of politicians and admirals in technical and operational matters. It was apparent from the outset, as indeed had been the case before the war, that Churchill gave himself the widest possible definition of his powers. The outbreak of hostilities led him ever deeper into planning details. He was restless, demanding, probing and imaginative. The rationale for his intervention lay in his conviction that the overall conduct of war was a matter for government. It also happened to be the case that Churchill gave more weight to his own strategic insights than to the advice he received from 'appropriate quarters'. Of course, this was not invariably the case, but the impression was frequently conveyed and inevitably led to friction with men who were under the impression that they possessed a professional expertise. It is not surprising that pre-war tensions were exacerbated in the heat of battle. The public expectation of a major naval triumph could not readily be met. The arrival of the German battle cruiser *Goeben* in Turkish territorial waters – and the impetus it gave to Ottoman intervention on the side of the Central Powers – was a blow to the simple notion that Britannia could easily rule the waves. The British success in the Battle of Heligoland Bight in August 1914 was not as great as Churchill liked to claim. It was also apparent, in the early months of the war, that the damage which German mines and submarines could cause had been underestimated. Captain Roskill, for example, also writes that 'Churchill's Board of Admiralty can hardly be acquitted of responsibility for the defenceless state of Scapa in 1914'.[3] Other writers have been less severe in their attribution of ministerial failure and have no fundamental criticism of Churchill in the early months of the war. There were setbacks and shortcomings but the navy remained in being for the crucial battles that might yet come.

In addition, there was the bonus afforded by Churchill's fertile imagination and readiness to question established procedures. For example, he speedily spotted the possibilities of 'Sigint' and the work of naval cryptographers. His interest in 'gadgets' was well-known. Some of these ideas came off and redounded to his credit; others seemed hairbrained and were forgotten, except by his critics. His interest in these matters clearly did not stem from a formed technological education but perhaps reflects the fact that in all spheres of knowledge he was largely self-taught. He did not observe the boundaries between disciplines which were built into a university education but cheerfully and sometimes crudely strode across them in pursuit of the unexpected. It may be, too, that this delight in surprise and his admiration for 'boffins' was a further expression of his belief that 'total war' was a 'great game' requiring ingenuity and cunning – a kind of extended public school 'prank'.

It was possible for Churchill to be respected by his naval and political colleagues and at the same time to be regarded as 'quite mad' – so long as no major disaster befell. The 'Antwerp affair' of October 1914 was an early indication that Churchill's behaviour could be described with almost equal appropriateness as ridiculous or heroic. The Belgian fortified port of Antwerp was under heavy German pressure in late September. If it fell, the Germans could advance upon Dunkirk, Calais and Boulogne. If its resistance was stiffened by a landing, there might be an opportunity to attack the exposed German flank. Churchill decided that only his personal presence could provide the necessary backbone. He reached Antwerp from Dunkirk in a Rolls-Royce and proceeded to tour the city, horn blaring, with a rifleman in the front seat to deal with emergencies.

This display was not without its effect on the gallant defenders but it made no difference to the outcome. It was an intervention which fell between two stools. The British assistance – Churchill himself apart – was on too small a scale to have made an effective defence possible. The Royal Naval Division's training and equipment were both defective. Even so, it is possible to argue that the intervention held up the German advance and secured the Channel ports for the Allies. This aspect, however, was rather obscured by Churchill's conduct in telegraphing Asquith offering to resign as First Lord of the Admiralty in order to take charge of the military operation in Antwerp. It was an offer which amazed his colleagues and which the Prime Minister declined. Churchill's behaviour confirmed the best and worst impressions. The First Lord was brave (foolhardy) and imaginative (impetuous) but he could hardly be a serious man of power.

The 'Antwerp Blunder' hastened the downfall not of Churchill but of the First Sea Lord, the German-born Prince Louis of Battenberg. He resigned shortly before a British naval defeat off the Chilean coast. Churchill decided to replace him by a 'terrific engine of mental and physical power', namely the seventy-three-year old Lord Fisher. It was an inescapably risky appointment. If naval matters improved, of course, it would appear inspired, but if difficulties developed critics would see the appointment as a further instance of Churchill's poor judgment of men. King George V was not alone in his doubts. Initially, however, the combination of two such mercurial men reassured the public. As he must have known would be the case, Churchill had to give the First Sea Lord great latitude. Together they initiated a new naval building programme. The British victory off the Falkland Islands in December 1914 gave the new partnership a splendid start. It was followed by the successful Battle of the Dogger Bank in January 1915. Churchill's political standing recovered perceptibly, but he did not draw the conclusion that the success had any connection with his own relative non-interference in operational matters.

The First Lord felt himself more free, under these circumstances, to speculate generally on the conduct of the war, being persuaded that offence was the best form of defence. From time to time he continued to contemplate various adventures in the North Sea – the occupation of the German island of Borkum, for example, would block the German navy's exit from its harbours and make possible an assault on Schleswig-Holstein. However, it was the entry of Ottoman Turkey into the war in November 1914 which caused Churchill to think again about the Near East. There were fears that an Ottoman army would attack the Suez Canal. At a meeting of the War Council on 25 November Churchill urged that the ideal method of defending Egypt would be by an attack on the Gallipoli Peninsula. However, it was not until the Russian appeal of 2 January for relief from Turkish pressure on the Caucasus that the idea of a Dardanelles 'demonstration' began to be taken seriously.

On Churchill's part, his enthusiasm for the scheme, which grew steadily, derived from a sense that neither side had sufficient strength to penetrate the other's lines in the Western theatre. Like other colleagues, he was casting around for a new objective. The War Council, skilfully addressed by Churchill on 13 January, resolved that the Admiralty should prepare for a naval expedition in February, to bombard and capture the Gallipoli Peninsula with Constantinople as its objective. Even at the outset, therefore, there was ambiguity and bad planning. Could the navy, unaided, seize the Peninsula or capture Constantinople? There were strong doubts on this score, not least from Fisher himself, but Churchill was full of enthusiasm and the old man, by this stage, was no match for Churchill's skill in argument and, somewhat mysteriously, failed to communicate the strength of his private feelings against the expedition to his colleagues. Was there to be a military force and if so, of what size? However, at this point, Kitchener, the Secretary of State for War, told the Cabinet shortly before the naval bombardment began on 19 February 1915 that no troops were immediately available for the Dardanelles. It was a further twist in the complex relationship between Churchill and Kitchener which had begun on the battlefields of the Sudan. Nevertheless, the bombardment went ahead – something for which Asquith and Churchill must share primary responsibility – but did not succeed. The delay in the release of troops was intensely irritating to Churchill, although he also paradoxically still hankered after a purely naval victory. It was vexing for him that the commander on the spot declined to repeat the attack which had come close to success on 18 March. The subsequent planning of the military landing was not Churchill's responsibility. It was to be Kitchener who controlled the military initiatives.

Churchill continued to make optimistic noises about the possibility of victory but his own position suddenly became very precarious. In the middle of May the relationship between Churchill and Fisher finally cracked. The First Sea Lord declared that he could not take part any longer in the Dardanelles 'foolishness' and threatened to depart for Scotland. Acknowledging the 'spite and malice' which would probably fall upon himself if the resignation went through, Churchill tried to get Fisher to change his mind, but failed. The crisis broadened, just at the point when Churchill thought that it was coming to an end and that he could remain at the Admiralty. It became clear to the Prime Minister that the Opposition would make great trouble if Churchill was left at the Admiralty and Fisher persisted in his resignation. In any event, Churchill, who had not been hostile to the notion of a Coalition government, now found himself caught in the manoeuvres which produced one –

though he did not sit idly by and merely wait for his political demise. Asquith proved unable or unwilling to retain for Churchill the post which the Conservatives were most anxious to deny him. He had to be content with the obscurity of the Chancellorship of the Duchy of Lancaster and membership of the newly-formed Dardanelles Committee. All might not yet be lost if the expedition eventually succeeded.

It is not difficult to find men gloating over Churchill's fall from grace. The Fisher/Churchill clash, obscure in its detail though it was, gave further ammunition to those who thought the First Lord an impossible person to work with. He clearly had some good ideas but he had little sense of proportion. Even though still only forty, it seemed to some political commentators that his career was finished. Meanwhile, as the Gallipoli campaign continued through the summer, Churchill's position became ever more untenable. The more he sought to defend his early decisions or advocate specific actions in the present, the more he became identified, by colleagues and a public anxious to find a scapegoat, as the chief architect of what was turning into a disaster. His opposition to the eventual evacuation came to look merely obstinate. Realising how weak his influence had become, Winston sought to escape from government altogether and pressed Asquith to give him a field command, but no offer was immediately forthcoming. When he was excluded from the War Committee, which replaced the Dardanelles Committee in November, Churchill formally resigned.

The Dardanelles campaign, the immediate cause of Churchill's fall, has been variously assessed over subsequent decades. In the inter-war period, in the light of the subsequent carnage on the Western Front and of Churchill's own defence of his actions in *The World Crisis*, commentators and historians looked more favourably upon the enterprise than had the Dardanelles Commission when it investigated matters in 1916. Subsequently, other writers have been less impressed. They have doubted whether victory was ever obtainable or even if it had been obtained doubted whether it would have drastically shortened the war against Germany. For such writers, it was an extravagant and bungled sideshow which should never have been contemplated. Assessments of Churchill's own role and responsibility have correspondingly fluctuated. Not surprisingly, perhaps, there appears to be a consensus that while Churchill was to blame for the shortcomings in initial conception and planning, he was not exclusively to blame. The machinery of government was inadequate for the demands placed upon it.

In the short term, however, the consequences for Churchill's own reputation were severe. Critics and enemies on other counts seized upon the Dardanelles. The lessons which Churchill himself drew are more difficult to discern. Both in his resignation speech in the Commons and in subsequent writing he was unrepentant – but very few politicians excuse themselves from the necessity of self-defence. Deep down, however, there was a private Churchill that was wounded and depressed by failure and rejection. Was there a fatal flaw in his make-up which would turn his brightest hopes to blank despair? Clementine Churchill had written to the Prime Minister on 20 May urging him not to part with Winston. He had spent nearly four years working to master every detail of naval science. No one could replace him. She ventured to suggest to Asquith that very few of his Cabinet possessed the power, the imagination and the deadliness to fight Germany which her husband possessed. She did not receive a reply. However, in the same month, the Prime Minister commented sadly on what he believed to be Winston's lack of proportion: 'To speak with the tongue of men and angels, and to spend laborious days and nights in administration, is no good if a man does not inspire trust.'[4] 'I knew everything', Churchill himself wrote subsequently, 'and could do nothing': there could not be a more graphic expression of the loss of power.[5] Yet, in his disappointment, Churchill drew one lesson. The First Lord of the Admiralty was indeed a powerful figure but he was not in the position of supreme power. 'I was ruined for the time being over the Dardanelles', he wrote, 'and a supreme enterprise was cast away, through my trying to carry out a major and combined operation of war from a subordinate position. Men are ill-advised to try such ventures.'[6] It remained to be seen whether the mistakes he had made in learning that lesson would confine him to a subordinate position for the rest of his life.

THE BORN SOLDIER 1915–1916

Margot Asquith, the Prime Minister's wife, was amongst those who fell to speculating on the subject of Winston Churchill at this juncture. His preeminence did not derive from intellect or judgment but from a unique combination of courage and colour. She found him longing to be in the trenches and dreaming of war and concluded that he was a born soldier. It was all very extraordinary.

Describing himself as 'the prodigal son', Churchill crossed to France on 18 November 1915 to join the Oxfordshire Hussars. However, the 'father' who saw him when he was still a great way off was Sir John French, the Commander-in-Chief, who invited him to dine and offered him the command of a brigade. Churchill insisted that he should first have experience of trench warfare and he was attached to the Grenadier Guards. It pleased him that the great Duke of Marlborough had once served in and commanded his battalion. He received a sullen welcome from his fellow-officers. He was told that a servant had been found for him who was carrying a spare pair of socks and his shaving gear. The rest of his kit had been left behind. Churchill insisted on experiencing life in the trenches for himself- and narrowly escaped death. He appeared to relish his new life and saluted his Commanding Officer as smartly as any. Yet he could not be an 'ordinary' soldier. He picked up political and military gossip from visitors and committed to paper his ideas on mobile shields which could be used in attack. When his mother offered to 'hot up' his friends in London on his behalf, Winston replied that his attitude towards the government should be called independent rather than hostile. Her tone should be salt, not bitter.

Even in France, politics caught up with him. Sir John French, whose personal position was precarious, repeated the offer of a brigade and Churchill was disposed to accept. However, unhappy about such a rapid elevation, Asquith intervened directly and vetoed the appointment. He had no objection, however, to a lesser position being offered and after a considerable delay Churchill found himself appointed – this time by Haig – to command the 6th Battalion, the Royal

Scots Fusiliers. Awaiting his appointment, it was not apparent to Churchill that a battalion commander would leave a mark in history. The realisation that he would not have a substantial military career, coupled with the correspondence he received from politicians in London, turned his thoughts back to politics. A Christmas visit to London, where he met Lloyd George, suggested a possible government crisis on the issue of compulsory service but Clementine warned against placing much confidence in Lloyd George – 'I assure you he is the direct descendent [sic] of Judas Iscariot'.[7] Churchill, however, was certain that his work with Asquith had come to an end. He had proved a weak and disloyal chief. It was in this mood that he returned to France and, at last, notification of his battalion.

That he was a very great admirer of the Scottish race was proved by his marriage, his constituency and now his regiment! He asked for a copy in one volume of the poems of Robert Burns to be sent out in order to soothe and cheer the spirits of his men, though he would not attempt to imitate their accent. His first impression was that the young officers were all 'small middle class Scotsmen' with no experience of soldiering. Their first impression was amazement that a well-known politician had suddenly appeared as their commanding officer. Churchill believed that a colonel, such as he now was, was an autocrat within his own sphere, who punished and promoted and displaced at his discretion. He told the officers that he would look after those who supported him and would break those who went against him. Such frankness was combined with a manifest concern for every detail in the life of the battalion which inspired confidence on the part of the men. So began several months in which Churchill applied himself zealously to soldiering 'up the line'. 'One lives calmly on the brink of the abyss', he wrote to Clementine on 20 February, 'But I can understand how tired people get of it if it goes on month after month. All the excitement dies away & there is only dull resentment.'[8]

There was less danger but more excitement in political London. While Churchill was quite willing to expatiate on the art of laying sandbags, he felt strongly within himself the feeling 'of knowledge and of power', as he put it in a letter to Max Aitken, his Canadian crony, which could be used to help in the direction of the war overall. His wife kept up a regular supply of political news and it was supplemented by comment from other quarters. The mood against Asquith was deepening, but could Lloyd George be trusted? The endless exchange of information rarely advanced beyond this encapsulation of the position.

Churchill returned to London on leave on 2 March, and unexpectedly decided to speak in the debate on the Navy Estimates, condemning what he regarded as the complacency of the Admiralty under Balfour. The surprise, however, was his concluding appeal for the restoration of Fisher as First Sea Lord. Winston apparently intended this suggestion as a gesture of reconciliation but it was widely interpreted as the act of a political adventurer, a clumsy gambler's throw for his own ends. Balfour's reply in the Commons was devastating. It was the 'folly' as much as the 'wickedness' of the statement which sank Churchill. Of course, he had been out of the country and had listened too uncritically to sympathetic journalists but he had once again misread a political situation.

He had been humiliated. Even so, on his return to his battalion, he continued to plan his political re-entry. He kept on telling himself that he would be quite content with the life of a soldier were it not for the fact that he felt himself fit for a wider scope. The suggestion that he needed a convincing motive for coming back from the front, made powerfully by his wife, fell on increasingly deaf ears as he dwelt on every hint of parliamentary crisis. Then, unexpectedly, the moment of decision arrived. The merger of battalions in his regiment, and his consequent loss of command, provided a plausible occasion to leave the army. The 'born soldier' had commanded in the field for just over four months.

. . .

CLIMBING BACK: MINISTER OF MUNITIONS
1917–1918

Churchill's return to political London was not in response to any clear signal. The way back looked hard and lonely. It is a measure of his commitment to power that he should have attempted it in such unpromising circumstances. Since office did not beckon, he sought income from journalism and relaxation from painting. Some comment in *The Times* and elsewhere suggested that he saw himself as leader of an

Opposition, merely waiting his chance. Churchill knew, however, that the best chance of rehabilitation lay in an investigation of the Dardanelles affair which might exonerate him or at least share his reponsibility with others. It was agreed in the summer of 1916 that a Commission should begin work under the chairmanship of Lord Cromer to investigate the Near Eastern imbroglio and Churchill devoted a good deal of time to preparing his own testimony for the Commission.

Kitchener's death at sea momentarily raised the possibility of a return to ministerial office, but Asquith acted as Secretary of State for War himself before appointing Lloyd George to this office. Churchill, holding Asquith to blame for the fact that the Dardanelles documents were not to be published, attacked the Prime Minister and criticised the strategy of the Somme offensive. He also returned to a favourite theme, that there was a vast African population which could be recruited. There were times when Churchill saw himself raising such a force personally. He also drew directly on his own front-line experience to draw attention to deficiencies in British equipment. Some of these points hit home, but the diffuse character of his remarks still conveyed the impression that his utterances were those of a disgruntled former naval person rather than the constructive comments of a man whose star was again rising. Occasional interesting tasks came his way – he agreed, for example, to draft a press statement on the outcome of the Battle of Jutland which was published under his own name. The request had come from Balfour! Despite such occasional signs of recognition, Churchill remained moody and out of sorts. It was during this period that Rothermere commissioned a portrait of him from the Irish painter Sir William Orpen. It revealed a man close to despair.

The only immediate way in which his career might be resurrected would be in the fall-out which might follow the collapse of the Asquith coalition; but there was no certainty even then. Churchill had convinced himself that if Lloyd George were to emerge as Prime Minister there would be a place for him in such a new government. In the event, his optimism again proved wide of the mark. In the complex manoeuvres which resulted in Asquith's downfall and Lloyd George's elevation, Churchill played little part. He was not in a position of power. To his bitter chagrin, he was not included in the new administration. The leading Tories made it clear that their own entry into the Cabinet was conditional on Churchill's exclusion. Lloyd George bowed before this pressure without undue difficulty. The new Prime Minister knew Churchill's good qualities more than most, but it probably quite suited him that he should establish himself in power before risking the challenge to his own leadership which Churchill might conceivably pose. As for Churchill himself, this time he was not merely disappointed. He was angry. Yet there was little that he could do. He was outside the government but in the divided Liberal Party he certainly did not count himself a devoted Asquithian admirer.

It was only in March 1917, when the First Report of the Dardanelles Commission was published, that his prospects brightened. Churchill was certainly not exonerated. He was accused of being carried away by his belief in the success of the operation in which he believed and of failing to ensure that naval advice was clearly put before the War Council. However, it was Asquith's handling of the War Council which was most severely censured. Kitchener was also criticised for delays in the despatch of troops. The outcome meant that the cry, 'What about the Dardanelles?', which had frequently assailed him, could no longer be directed against him exclusively. His political rehabilitation became a possibility. He looked to Lloyd George to act.

The Prime Minister did not find it easy. Conservative opposition was still fierce and was not easily reconciled to Lloyd George's proposition that it was better to have Churchill, an increasingly effective speaker in the Commons, as an ally rather than an opponent. It took considerable manoeuvering before Churchill's appointment as Minister of Munitions was announced on 17 July. *The Morning Post* was not alone in predicting fresh colossal blunders at the cost of the nation from this apparently unsinkable minister. While some of Churchill's correspondents regretted that he had not received a post commensurate with his ability, wiser voices urged him this time to stick to munitions and not try to run the entire government. In fact, the extent of opposition to his appointment may even have given Churchill pause. Even more, he appreciated that he was beholden to the Prime Minister who would be likely to rein him in sharply if he sought a major role. This time, there was no doubt that Lloyd George had the power. Their lengthy relationship did not mean that theirs was an equal partnership. Yet the factors which had made their unlikely alliance so potent a decade earlier had not entirely disappeared. There were even times when Churchill could see that if the Prime Minister kept him under control it was for his own good. The fruitful exercise of power required restraint and discipline, neither of which came easily to Churchill. However, the fact that he was not a member of the War Cabinet inevitably circumscribed his sphere of operations.

Churchill's appointment required him to submit himself to the electors of Dundee since an Independent candidate was not to be deterred by the truce between the main parties. Although he had recently received the freedom of the city, it could not be said that his constituency had seen much of him in recent years. The brief campaigning that he undertook, before leaving matters largely in the hands of his wife, revealed a degree of discontent which Churchill had hitherto not directly experienced in the war. He held the seat comfortably, but his opponent's poll was not derisory. The downfall of the Tsar was only one sign of a war-weariness which was beginning to emerge throughout Europe. Churchill firmly rejected the idea of peace by negotiation but the existence of a changing mood lent fresh urgency to the effort to achieve victory in which he would now be called upon to play a significant part.

At the Ministry of Munitions, the post which he held until the end of the war, Churchill initially had an administrative task to attend to. His immediate predecessors had found themselves increasingly immersed in detailed issues which might more effectively be handled by a supervisory board. He set up a 'Munitions Council' under his chairmanship, serviced by a proper secretariat. He reported to the Prime Minister that he was delighted 'with all these clever business men' who were helping him to their utmost. It was the first time that he had come into working contact with men from such a background. Less harmonious were his dealings with the Admiralty. It was almost inevitable that there would be some clashes with the First Lord since Churchill could not resist offering some observations on naval armaments even though his ministry was responsible for munitions for the army only. On production issues Churchill found himself to some extent back in the world of industrial relations which he had first encountered at the Board of Trade. Commissions of Enquiry into unrest in industrial districts had concluded that one of the chief causes of industrial discontent was 'dilution', the erosion of wage differentials between skilled and unskilled workers. In an attempt to meet the grievances of the skilled, Churchill proposed a substantial percentage increase for them, a step which predictably caused discontent among the unskilled. Clearly, the Minister of Munitions did not solve this problem but he did prevent major industrial disruption, with the grave consequences it would have had for munitions manufacture. Although concerned, by 1918, about the continuing evidence of discontent, his negotiating stance in industrial disputes somewhat belied the reputation for truculence which he had gained in his time as Home Secretary.

Throughout his period at Munitions, Churchill took a generous view of his need to visit France, ostensibly to see the requirements of the army at first hand but in practice to form for himself a general view of the progress of the war. The Prime Minister was prepared to listen to his observations. In January 1918, for example, he warned of the dangers of a German spring offensive. It was vital to increase shells, aeroplanes and tanks. He became increasingly obsessed by the need to create a mechanically superior army. He wanted to wait until 1919 before launching an offensive and achieving the longed-for 'knock-out blow' with tanks. His views on these matters were listened to with respect but not adopted in full. The scenario was by now a familiar one. Winston frequently perceived the potential of equipment, and a style of warfare to make use of it, ahead of most men but he was apt to minimise the operational difficulties in the short term.

Churchill happened to be at the front in March 1918 on the day before the German attack began. The scale of the bombardment alarmed but did not surprise him. He hurried back to London and urgently implemented plans to speed up munitions production to cope with the emergency which he had correctly forecast. Men and munitions should be carried to France by all means and with all speed. One of the specific measures which he also advocated was the immediate extension of conscription to Ireland. It was a measure of his capacity to respond without panic to a crisis that Lloyd George decided to send him to France both to assess the situation and to urge upon the French government the necessity for a vigorous attack. In these days in late March Churchill was again in his element. He found himself at the heart of decision-making in a manner which he could scarcely have thought likely a year earlier.

It was predictable that this experience recharged Winston's enthusiasm for the consideration of wider issues. The functioning of government was particularly on his mind. After a conversation with the Prime Minister, he sent a letter on 4 May in which he expressed his willingness to give his advice when it was asked for but he was not willing to undertake any responsibility for policy – a pointed remark in the context of an imminent attack on Lloyd George in the Commons. This arose out of the allegations of Sir Frederick Maurice that the Prime Minister had attempted to starve Haig of troops in the winter of 1917–18. The existing system placed that burden upon the War Cabinet alone. In these circumstances he stressed that he would never acccept political responsibility without recognised regular power. It was time to set up a Cabinet again which would be able to consider policy issues independently of the War Cabinet. In a further memorandum he pointed out that the present arrangement did not make it possible to build up any new effective party machinery. It was an observation of relevance to his own long-term political future as well as the Prime Minister's, but Lloyd George apparently chose not to reply to these suggestions. There was undoubtedly sense in them, but the only way to keep Winston from bombarding him with ideas was to ignore a good proportion of them.

In any case, over the summer, Churchill was soon diverted back to France where he was enthralled by the progress of the fighting. He took the view that his own work made it necessary for him to keep continually in touch with the conditions on the spot. It was a view of his duty which was not universally shared. The House of Commons scarcely saw him for months. Churchill pounced on every successful use of the tank as justification for his own ambitious plans for mechanical warfare in 1919. Back in Britain, he visited the main centres of munitions production, again with the intention of preparing for the great offensive which was to come in 1919. By October, however, it was becoming evident that the war might actually come to an end without the advanced campaign on which Winston had set his heart. After a final

CHURCHILL

visit to the front, he managed to be back in his office in the Hotel Metropole looking towards Trafalgar Square at 11 am on 11 November 1918. 'After fifty-two months of making burdens grievous to be borne', he wrote later in *The World Crisis*, 'and binding them on men's backs, at last, all at once, suddenly and everywhere the burdens were cast down.'

The burden of wartime office was in fact one which Churchill had relished rather than endured. Although he had referred, during his brief sojourn as a soldier, to the great relief he derived from his lack of ministerial responsibility, his remarks are not very persuasive. During his gloomy months in 1916 he fretted at his absence from power at this juncture of all junctures. He could offer more in war than he could in a hundred years of peace. In the event, he had bounced back from disaster but even so he could only be said to have had a 'mixed' war. He had become an even more contentious figure than he had been in 1914. Both his brilliance and his clumsiness became more transparent. Despite suggestions in some quarters in 1914 that the First Lord of the Admiralty would be the man to win the war, he had in fact ended it in a subordinate position to Lloyd George – upon whom now all things depended, or so it seemed.

. . .

IN COALITION: 1919–1922

Lloyd George's position in December 1918 was paradoxical. His conduct of the war gave him enormous prestige, but his political base was weak, except in the short term. He remained a Liberal but required and received Conservative support to survive. He believed that he could maintain that Coalition into the peace. There was no possibility of a swift Liberal reunion.

Churchill's options were determined by the Prime Minister's strategy. He too decided that the maintenance of the Coalition made sense. The victory was national. It did not belong to any party or class. The peace should likewise be made by a government with wide cross-party support. This appeal was persuasive – and it was also particularly convenient for Churchill. As Minister of Munitions, he had gained some sense of the mood of industrial workers. There was a desire for change which the Labour Party, at last, might capture. It was already apparent that most of its leaders, now that peace had arrived, were determined to fight as an independent entity. Labour might make rapid political progress and transform the nature of British party politics. If this should turn out to be the case, there were alternative possibilities: the parties currently forming the Coalition could formally fuse: the Liberals could reunite: the Conservatives could go their own way: a new Centre Party could be born. In such circumstances, it was not clear where Churchill would find a political home.

Immediately, however, there was no apparent cause for anxiety. In the December 1918 General Election the Coalition received a massive endorsement. There were nearly five times as many Liberal MPs supporting Lloyd George as opposing him, but the Coalition Unionists were by far the largest party. Overall, the Liberal share of the vote had halved since the last election in 1910. Asquith lost his seat. So did the most prominent Labour leaders, though the party as a whole made some progress. The result was all the more surprising, at least to some observers, because the election was fought under the provisions of the new Representation of the People Act which gave the vote to all adult males, without any property qualification, and to women over thirty, with a property or marital qualification. It was a very different electorate from the one on which Edwardian party politics had rested. 'The only uncertain element', Churchill wrote to his wife from Dundee during his own campaign, 'is the great one, this enormous electorate composed of so many of the poorest people in the country'.[9] It was also the case that Asquith had many admirers among the Dundee Liberals. He was confident, however, that he would head the poll in what was a two-member constituency, and so it proved. There were, nonetheless, some worrying features. Of course, no Conservative candidate stood: what would happen if and when one did? Labour took the other seat, but the Independent Prohibitionist candidate, an old opponent, polled well. The triumph notwithstanding, Dundee was no longer a safe seat for a Liberal.

The Liberalism which Churchill offered the electorate had as much right to that title as any other being offered in 1918. He saw himself as still 'progressive' and indeed the local newspaper claimed that the Prime Minister would find in him his 'strongest lieutenant' on this wing of his administration. Churchill promised, for example, something he could not deliver, namely the nationalisation of the railways. It had been one of his enthusiasms for a decade. He waxed indignant about individuals who had made fortunes out of the war. His rhetoric sought to adapt for peace the language used in war. It would be folly to throw away the experience of 'concerted effort by all classes' and descend into bickering, class jealousies and 'Party froth' which would produce privation. He expressed contempt for all who had been defeatist during the war or who had advocated peace by negotiation. He talked also about the need to assure 'the great mass of the toilers' of 'decent minimum standards of life and labour'. His criticism of Socialism remained strong but there should be 'just laws' which would regulate the acquisition of wealth. Here was a rewarming of themes from Board of Trade days, to be given fresh vitality by patriotic seasoning. In detail,it was not clear what any of it meant or whether it would have much relationship to the programme of the Coalition government.

In the days before the Armistice, when Lloyd George was already fashioning his plans for a continuance of the Coalition, Churchill again gave the Prime Minister the benefit of his views on the degradation of being a Minister without responsibility for policy. On the other hand, it was well known in the Prime Minister's entourage that Winston felt even more strongly the degradation of not being a Minister at all. Once more, Winston was in danger of pressing his luck too far in appearing to seek to know how the new government was to be constituted before declaring his own willingness to serve. Lloyd George would not be drawn into specific commitments on the kind of Cabinet system he would run. Churchill, in turn, was not averse to supplying the Prime Minister with copious advice on the membership of a Cabinet. He himself hankered after a return to the Admiralty, and it was an initial possibility, but after a few days he accepted reluctantly that this could not be. Instead, he was designated Secretary of State for War and Air, to the accompaniment of predictable criticism from sections of the Conservative press. It was a pivotal position at a time when the Great War had ended but when Europe was still far from peaceful. Issues of power again came to the fore. What kind of power was Great Britain in the world of 1919? What challenges and difficulties could be predicted? And what power did Churchill personally possess to fashion appropriate policies?

To some extent, for all those ministers engaged in directing the war effort, victory had become an end in itself and Churchill shared the general surprise that it ended when it did. Of course, from time to time, 'war aims' had been promulgated in public and there had been innumerable plans and secret diplomatic manoeuvres at various stages in the conflict. Churchill had discovered early on that the war was in defence of 'Christian civilisation' and did not extensively stray in public from this basic insight. His responsibilities had never directly embraced the formulation of specific objectives. In 1918, however, as rumours circulated about a negotiated peace, he had been quick to dismiss any such possibility. Any settlement with Germany would be a mistake unless the Germans had been 'definitely worsted'.

Churchill's correspondent, his cousin, Ivor Guest, had suggested that whatever accumulation of German power there might in the end be in a negotiated settlement, it would be 'more than set off by the English speaking solidarity'. Certainly, Churchill welcomed that solidarity and did all he could to extend it. He told a meeting of the Anglo-Saxon Fellowship on 4 July 1918 that he experienced emotions which words could not describe when he watched 'the splendour of American manhood' striding forward in France and Flanders. Britain's reward for her action in 1914, he claimed, was the 'supreme reconciliation' of Britain and the United States.[10] He chose not to dwell on the tardiness of American intervention or the extent to which the US administration still distanced itself from the commitments entered into by the Allies. 'English speaking solidarity' was a fine phrase but the working out of the supposed 'supreme reconciliation' might be troublesome.

At least temporarily, the war had made Churchill a European. His visits to France and his soldiering gave him an intimate feeling and affection for the country. In Clemenceau he found a man comparably indifferent to danger at the front. Churchill had a certain idea of France, even if he expressed it in bad French. However, it was clear to him that the German question remained central to the future of Europe. He did not distinguish between the German government and the German nation when it came to the cause of the war: 'they were all in it'. As a consequence, he believed Alsace-Lorraine ought to be returned to France. Yet, while Germany ought to be and would be punished, a certain magnanimity would be prudent. Such concern did not stem primarily from any ardent desire for reconciliation but rather from a concern for the fevered internal condition of Germany and the possibility of a revolution which would bring the Bolshevik bacillus closer to the heart of Europe. To allow policy to be based upon the understandable emotion of the moment, where Germany was concerned, without regard to the future balance of power in Europe, would be folly.

It was with Bolshevism that Churchill was most concerned. His language about the threat it posed varied in metaphor in the months that followed but was never less than colourful. He had a vision of an evil tyranny stretching from Japan into the heart of Europe. He thought Bolsheviks had been interrupting his meetings in Dundee. The Bolshevik tyranny was the worst tyranny in history. The strength of this conviction led to the view among those who considered themselves balanced that he was obsessive on the subject. Churchill's own perspective owed a good deal to the secret intelligence material which came his way after British cryptographers had broken Russian codes. More generally, however, it was a matter of intuition. He favoured a liberal constitutional development in Russia and was appalled by the character of the regime the Bolsheviks were seeking to impose. He was not in a position to determine what British policy should be, but his office naturally drew him to a considerable extent into the discussion. There were already British forces (and some drawn from other nationalities) inside Russia from 1917 with a confused mission to prevent facilities and equipment falling into German hands and possibly to re-establish an Eastern Front. If they remained, they might be drawn into the Russian Civil War even more than was already the case. But perhaps they ought not only to be drawn in but to be strengthened and supplemented with a view to defeating Bolshevism?

Churchill thought so, at least in the early months of 1919, though his own enquiries revealed a reluctance on the part of soldiers to fight in Russia. He came to the view that only Russian armies could defeat the Bolsheviks but they needed support and encouragement if they were to succeed. Lloyd George, however, had two objections which he considered decisive. He did not believe that the Russian generals who might be assisted were liberal democrats. Secondly, he quoted historical precedents to suggest that foreign intervention would prove counter-productive. He also feared the expense. Decision-making on this complex matter was frequently complicated by the absence of the Prime Minister or Foreign Secretary at the Peace Conference in Paris. Churchill fulminated against a policy of drift and watched the steady growth of Bolshevik authority with dismay. He accused colleagues, not least the Prime Minister, of betraying those Russians who were still seeking to resist its complete consolidation. He succeeded in getting some additional aid for Denikin in mid-August, but by the end of October the last British troops were withdrawn from Archangel and Murmansk. Churchill appeared to have plausible grounds, indeed, for believing that Denikin could achieve a victory. However, in the months that followed, the government more and more distanced itself from internal events in Russia. Churchill was dismayed and disgusted by what he regarded as the spinelessness of his colleagues in this matter.

Churchill could not understand why his stance on this issue led him to be thought 'reactionary'. Since he had a high regard for the principle of monarchy it is not surprising that he had a rather soft-hearted conception of the last Tsar. However, his main complaint remained that Bolshevism was imposed on Russia by force. Left to themselves, the Russian people would not have voted for such a system. If the Allies stood aside, the Russian people and they themselves might have to pay a heavy price in the future for the failure to crush Bolshevism in its cradle.

The difficulty with such a vision was that it required men to fight and a nation to endorse such an effort. In his grand perception of what needed to be done, Churchill seemed almost oblivious to the fact that a Great War had just come to an end and the great majority of the population did not share his willingness to start all over again, even supposing the cause was sound. Yet his own experience of demobilisation told him that very clearly.

The British Army at the end of the war was a vastly different force from that which had existed in 1914. If it survived in its existing condition it would be a serious factor in the European power balance. But no one thought it could or should survive. National Service had been an aberration made necessary only by the exigencies of war. Millions of conscripts now wanted to resume normal life as soon as possible. On taking office, faced with evidence of insubordination and mutiny in Britain and France, Churchill decided to scrap the existing proposals for demobilisation. A new scheme, based upon age, length of service and injury proved more acceptable and lessened tension. Conscription was retained until 1920, but some two and a half million men were released. Rapid demobilisation was an inevitable response to social and economic pressure, but it prevented any serious and sustained examination of what kind of army a Great Power like Britain required in order to sustain its role in the world. Was the lesson of the previous quarter of a century that Britain only needed a volunteer army of a quarter of a million men? It was not the case, however, that Churchill struggled in vain with his colleagues for such a comprehensive review. The Cabinet agreed in August 1919, on his initiative, that the British Empire would not be engaged in any great war during the next ten years and that no Expeditionary Force would be required. The Service Estimates were framed on these assumptions.[11]

It could be argued that air power might become a substitute for manpower. Churchill's enthusiasm for flying was one reason why it seemed to make sense to tag 'Air' on to 'War' in his brief. There were early complaints, however, that Churchill was not giving this side of his responsibilities sufficient attention. One solution which appealed to him was the appointment of a Minister of Defence with four subordinate departments – War, Admiralty, Air and Supply (formerly Munitions). Perhaps because Churchill made it apparent that he would be an admirable candidate for such a post, it was not proceeded with. However, he was persuaded that the Royal Air Force, as it became known, should be an independent force rather than one subordinated to the two older services. There were many battles fought to sustain that position. Churchill was profoundly convinced that air power would profoundly alter the strategy of the future, but had scarcely been able to give this question the attention it deserved.

One reason why he could not was the increasing gravity and hopelessness of the Irish situation. Overall policy in

Ireland was not a matter for him, but the provision of troops was. The 1916 Easter Rising, followed by the dominant Sinn Fein showing (outside Ulster) in the UK General Election of 1918, produced a situation in Ireland very different in character from the time in 1913–14 when Churchill had last been closely involved. Then he had been the target of Unionist criticism for his willingness to threaten them with coercion. In 1919–20 it was his willingness not only to authorise the despatch of regular troops to Southern Ireland but to countenance irregular activities which brought him increasing opprobrium, at least in Liberal circles. His approach rested on the premise that there had to be a 'trial of strength' from which would issue the chance of a settlement on wider lines. He was prepared to recruit a substantial force of Ulstermen who would operate not only in the province but throughout Ireland. Here was a reflection of his belief that a government which met violence and insurrection half-heartedly and inadequately lacked a proper understanding of the use of power. A tentative response, which might seem admirable, only prolonged the agony. His willingness to countenance reprisals and his acceptance of the military belief that Martial Law in certain Irish counties would succeed disturbed his wife. She urged moderation, adding 'It always makes me unhappy & disappointed when I see you *inclined* to take for granted that the rough, iron-fisted "Hunnish" way will prevail'.[12] Her letter was dated 18 February 1921. Three days earlier, he had left the War Office and taken up his new responsibility as Colonial Secretary. The advice, however, was of equal relevance in his new post.

Churchill had been thrilled by the response of the British Empire as a whole to the war. Although his own passion for raising an East African force had never been realised, he interpreted the contribution from the scattered territories of the Crown, both dependent and self-governing, as testimony to the value and vitality of the imperial system. He praised the advisory role of General Smuts, the erstwhile Boer commander in the South African War, for example, as an illustration of its capacity to absorb and transform previous conflicts. He knew that the 'Dominions' would take an early opportunity, after the war, to seek clarification of their constitutional status. While he never welcomed any moves which might undermine the intimate association which he believed the Empire to be, it seemed likely that greater autonomy could be conceded amicably within a framework which preserved the essence of the relationship.

He did not anticipate any comprehensive challenge to the British Empire from subject peoples whether in West Africa, the West Indies, or Malaya, to name only three distinct regions. His own pre-1914 experiences did not suggest that the extension of self-government in such areas was either necessary or desirable, either from the standpoint of ruler or of ruled. He was so confident of British superiority that he only occasionally felt any need to place it on a supposedly 'racial' footing. Even so, he was aware that the current of opinion was beginning to move against the kind of Imperialism which had existed before 1914. The colonies stripped from Germany and parts of the erstwhile Ottoman Empire had not been directly annexed by victorious countries. They were 'mandated' to administer them under the aegis of the new League of Nations and, where the territories concerned were more 'advanced', to prepare them for self-government. Churchill naturally believed in the League of Nations because it was not politically safe to do otherwise. It was not clear how this new organisation would develop but its notional responsibilities in the colonial area were a sign of a changing perspective concerning colonialism.

It was also disconcerting that in 1917, the Secretary of State for India, Edwin Montagu, had committed the government to greater Indian participation in the government of India. There was to be 'responsible government...as an integral part of the British Empire'. These changes, limited though they were, had been put in hand in 1919. Churchill spoke strongly on the government's behalf in the fierce debate in the Commons that followed the disciplining of General Dyer for the 'Amritsar Massacre' in India in 1919 – when troops had fired on a crowd – but he was not a little alarmed when in the same debate Montagu denounced 'the ascendancy of one race over another'. Churchill himself held no such principle, but he did believe that it was incumbent upon the ruling race to conduct itself with restraint and to use its power, so far as possible, in the interests of the governed. Such notions seemed to him eminently defensible. They sprang from his experience of Asia and Africa. He knew that there were backward races in the world with no capacity for self-government. It was irresponsible and absurd to suppose that democratic institutions could be granted to them successfully.

He therefore came to the Colonial Office without apology. He knew that he had no direct responsibility for India in his new post but was well aware of the effect of whatever might be decided on the future of the sub-continent. He told a Council of Ministers in February 1922 that he was strongly opposed to the view, which he found to be prevalent among many people both at home and in India, that Britain was fighting a rearguard action in India and that the raj was doomed. It was in this spirit that he braced himself for the challenges that confronted him.

The overlap between his previous and his new responsibilities was considerable. The pressures in favour of economy again operated powerfully. It was believed that order in the Empire would be greatly facilitated by the advent of air power. Indeed Churchill had acknowledged that 'the first duty of the Royal Air Force is to garrison the British Empire', and he continued as Air Minister for some months after he left the War Office. Mesopotamia (Iraq), newly mandated to Britain, could be very economically controlled by this means. It was also necessary to ensure the compliance of local rulers both in Iraq and Transjordan (which was to be separated from Palestine). Churchill had already noted the problems caused by the fact that territories under British control in the Middle East were variously looked after by the Colonial Office, the Foreign Office and the India Office. He saw that the solution to these overlapping jurisdictions lay in the creation of a Middle East Department which would deal with all of the territories. It would come under the control of the Colonial Secretary.

The new minister could not resist the urge to travel to the Middle East and called a major conference in Cairo to discuss the region's problems with the officials concerned. The reception he received from sections of Egyptian opinion was a reminder that the attempts to settle that country's status had not yet been successful. Churchill, however, was more interested in going to Jerusalem, where he endeavoured to explain to interested parties precisely what Britain aimed to do in Palestine. His speeches envisaged a prosperous and cooperative future for both Jews and Arabs. The principles of the 1917 Balfour Declaration – which had promised the Jews a 'national home' in Palestine – could not be departed from, but he was certain that the cause of Zionism would also bring with it prosperity, contentment and advancement to the Arab population of the country. There was little exceptionable in the sentiments expressed. What was lacking was an understanding of the limited capacity of the British government to control developments which their own policies had set in train. In the short term, however, from a British point of view, Churchill's crystallisation of the boundaries and jurisdictions in the Middle East could be judged a success.[13]

The other major problem which did not go away with his change of post was Ireland, but his attitude did change. By the late spring of 1921 he was urging a truce so that talks could begin. Lloyd George himself was the major figure in the negotiations, but when the 'Articles of Agreement for a Treaty' of December 1921 envisaged Dominion status for the new Irish Free State, it fell to Churchill to take charge of the transfer of power in Ireland. It was no easy task in an atmosphere of continuing suspicion, terror and impending civil war. It fell to Churchill too to try to head off Tory diehard criticism of the outcome in Ireland.

It was a combination of Tory discontent arising out of the Irish problem and unhappiness at Lloyd George's handling of the 'Chanak crisis' of 1922 which precipitated the downfall of the Coalition government. The Prime Minister had consistently supported the Greek cause in Asia Minor since 1918. Conscious of Britain's Moslem subjects, Churchill had never liked the policy. In August 1922, however, when Turkish forces approached the allied forces in the neutral zone covering Constantinople, having earlier defeated Greek forces, Churchill supported the Prime Minister's order to the Turks to stop. The country again faced the prospect of war. Conservative ministers resigned following a meeting of Conservative MPs at the Carlton Club on 19 October 1922. Lloyd George could not go on as Prime Minister. It was time for the country to deliver its verdict as the political parties fragmented and the future looked uncertain. It looked as though there was a yearning for the return of 'normalcy' and the drawing of a line under the war and war-in-peace which had lasted since 1914.

NOTES AND REFERENCES

1. Winston S. Churchill, *The World Crisis, 1911–1918* Vol I, London, 1938, p.153.
2. Randolph S. Churchill, *Winston S. Churchill*, Volume II, *The Young Statesman 1901–1914*, London, 1967, pp. 710–11.
3. Stephen Roskill, *Churchill and the Admirals*, London, 1977, p. 35.
4. Martin Gilbert, *Winston S. Churchill*, Volume III, *1914–1916*, London, 1971, pp. 459–60.
5. *Ibid.* p. 742.
6. Cited and discussed in Robert Rhodes James, *Churchill: a Study in Failure 1900–1939*, London, 1970, pp. 86–8.
7. Gilbert, *op.cit.*, p. 623.
8. *Ibid.* p. 675.
9. Gilbert, *Winston S. Churchill*, Volume IV, *1917–1922*, London, 1975, p. 172.
10. *Ibid.* p. 122.
11. H. M. Pelling, *Winston Churchill*, London, 1974, pp. 276–7.
12. Gilbert, *op.cit.*, p. 471.
13. See J.G. Darwin, *Britain, Egypt and the Middle East: Imperial Policy in the Aftermath of war, 1918–1922*, London, 1981, and Keith Jeffrey, *The British Army and the Crisis of Empire, 1918–1922*, Manchester, 1984, for a general discussion of the issues with which Churchill had to deal.

Chapter 4

DOWN AND OUT?
1922–1939

. . .

EXILE: 1922–1924

Churchill's defeat at Dundee in the November 1922 General
Election came as a heavy blow. He was out of parliament for
the first time in twenty-two years and it looked as though his
career was in ruins. An operation for appendicitis weakened
him and he was only able to appear in the constituency at the
very end of the campaign. His wife spoke valiantly on his
behalf, though she was disconcerted to find her pearls spat
upon by Dundee women. A drunken and intemperate speech
on his behalf by F.E. Smith may explain why Churchill was
swept to defeat on a torrent of prohibition. Scrymgeour, his
veteran Independent opponent, headed the poll. E.D. Morel,
organiser of the Union of Democratic Control, who stood for
Labour, was also elected. Churchill's vote was well down and
he came in fourth. 'The Scotch electorate', wrote Lord
Stamfordham from Buckingham Palace, 'is rather an incomprehensible body.'[1] What is perhaps more incomprehensible,
however, is that Churchill's political base should ever have
been a city with whose inhabitants he had so little in common.
Three weeks of campaigning at election times had sufficed in
the past. On this occasion, he had not been able to oblige.
Even when fully fit, however, he would be unwise to fight
again in Dundee.

He might be unwise to fight anywhere. He was now forty-
eight. Despite recurring premonitions of death, he was now
older than Lord Randolph had been when when he died.

88

War-wounded friends were dying young. He was beginning to have mellow middle-aged reflections. His youngest daughter died. Yet he had three young children of whom he was distantly fond and who might demand of him more than an occasional reluctant outing to an East Coast beach. He might allow his wife, who stood by him so conscientiously, more of his time. He had recently purchased Chartwell, a house in Kent. An inheritance temporarily eased his financial problems. He could continue to paint and there were memoirs to write. He could even still play polo.

It was not only that private life might have positive attractions, at least after a four-month holiday in the Mediterranean. The political scene beyond Dundee was murky. The national result showed a striking advance for Labour (142 MPs compared with 59 in 1918) which put the party ahead of 117 Liberals (approximately equally divided between followers of Asquith and Lloyd George). The Conservatives had a majority of 88 over the other parties. Even supposing that the Liberals could overcome their divisions, it was difficult to envisage that they would form a government of their own in the future. Although it was difficult to believe that Lloyd George would never again hold office, for the moment at least he had been eclipsed by the 'unknown' Prime Minister, Bonar Law. Churchill was as much a 'personality' in politics as Lloyd George and for the moment shared in the obloquy attaching to such a defect. The advice of Margot Asquith was that he should 'lie low' and do nothing in politics but go on writing all the time. Painting, too, had much to recommend it. It would become apparent in time whether and how he should seek to re-enter the House of Commons.

The writing, journalism apart, consisted of the war memoirs on which he had embarked while still a Cabinet Minister. The controversies of the war made it inevitable that participants, sooner or later, would seek to present their side of the story. Even the reticent Lord Grey of Fallodon appeared in print. Churchill, however, was ahead of the pack, and his zeal in this respect provoked a crisis concerning official secrecy and access to material. The result of his heavy labours was *The World Crisis*, the first volume of which appeared in 1923. Subsequent volumes came on stream in steady succession. The fifth and last appeared in 1931, in which year there was also published an abridged and revised single volume. This publication history ensured that Churchill's name was kept before the public as a writer, whatever else befell him.

It was unkindly suggested that Churchill wrote five volumes about himself and called the product *The World Crisis*. Certainly this title contributed to the substantial sales in a way that an alternative title, *The Great Amphibian*, helpfully suggested by Geoffrey Dawson, the editor of *The Times*, where it was serialised, would not have done. It reflected the philosophical pretensions of the work. Not unnaturally, Churchill set out to place his own actions in a favourable light. It is not difficult, in the light of subsequent memoirs and of access to documents, for historians to draw attention to omissions, distortions and misplaced emphases which at this juncture detract from its 'objective' value.[2]

To dwell on such shortcomings, however, would be to overlook its significance as a statement about national, international and personal power. The successive volumes provided an implicit commentary on the politics of the post-war period. The first two volumes, however, in Cowling's words, struck a note that was 'powerful and energetic'.[3] The language – which Churchill dictated – conveyed his sense of an epic contest. The struggle in the North Sea between such massive forces was 'the culminating manifestation of naval force in the history of the world'. The stirring quality of the early encounters, when Churchill himself was still in charge, had not yet been superseded by the grim and debilitating grind of the later years. It was a perspective which did not march easily with the sombre mood of Britain in 1923.

Baldwin's decision in November to go to the country on the ground that protection was the only way to fight unemployment forced Churchill off the fence. He declared publicly that such a move would delay the return of prosperity and diminish the influence of the British Empire as an agent of reconciliation on the European continent. He stood in West Leicester but was defeated by the middle-class Labour candidate, F.W. Pethick-Lawrence, and only came in front of the Conservative candidate by quite a small margin. Overall, the Liberals made a modest recovery in their defence of Free Trade, but, even so, the Labour Party kept well ahead. The Conservatives remained the largest of the three parties. In these circumstances, after Baldwin lost a vote of no-confidence, in January 1924 Ramsay MacDonald formed the first

Labour government, an administration which would depend upon Liberal support for its survival.

Churchill was disappointed by this outcome, for he would have preferred Asquith to have formed a government with Conservative support. His own campaign at Leicester had become increasingly anti-Labour rather than anti-Conservative. The advent of a Labour government was an unpalatable shock. It confirmed his analysis of the linkage between domestic and international developments. In moments akin to despair, he saw the enemies of Britain consorting together at home and abroad to achieve its destruction. 'Britain will never consent . . .', he had written to the Archbishop of Tuam at the end of 1920 'to the destruction of the integrity of the British Empire.'⁴ In a speech he described Ireland as 'the heart's centre of the British Empire' – but Ireland had been 'lost'. In 1922, too, Egypt had been declared 'independent', a step which, while more nominal than real, indicated the trend of the times. And now, Socialism had come to Westminster. It was the kind of serious national misfortune which usually only befell great states on the morrow of defeat in war and it threatened to cast a shadow over every form of national life and confidence. It was in vain that attempts were made to distinguish between Socialism as the Labour Party understood it and as the Bolsheviks understood it. There were turbulent currents flowing beneath the moderate exterior.

It was suspected in various newspapers that Winston was preparing the way to return to the party he had left – the Conservatives. Amidst a certain amount of manoeuvring on the Conservative side, Churchill stood as an 'Independent Anti-Socialist' at a by-election in the Abbey Division of Westminster in March 1924 and was only narrowly defeated by the Conservative candidate. The Liberal vote collapsed completely. Churchill was advised from various quarters to preserve a detached position from the Tory Party until the time was ripe to discuss the terms for re-admission. On 7 May 1924, however, Churchill addressed a Conservative rally in Liverpool organised by Archibald Salvidge, the dominant Tory figure in local government on Merseyside. By September, after a summer of signs and signals between Churchill and the Tory hierarchy, he was addressing a Conservative rally in Edinburgh on the subject of the Socialist threat, and had been adopted for the Epping Division which he was to fight at the next General Election as a 'Constitutionalist' (with Conservative support).

That event came more quickly than had been anticipated following the defeat of the government in the Commons in early October. In the ensuing contest, Churchill romped home, comfortably defeating a Liberal opponent, with Labour a poor third. His language about Socialism grew more strident with every succeeding speech, and his diagnosis of the threat it posed was strengthened by the supposed 'Zinoviev Letter', a communication which purported to come from the President of the Comintern in Moscow to the British Communist party calling for armed struggle against capitalism and sedition among the forces of the Crown. It was published four days before polling. Nationally, the Conservatives gained a clear overall majority and Baldwin was in a position to form a government which, in contrast to the instability of the previous few years, would be likely to last its term. Churchill had been out of parliament for two years, but after his victory he successfully applied to join the Conservative Party. He had been absent from its ranks for twenty years.

· · ·

CHANCELLOR OF THE EXCHEQUER: 1924–1929

It was not only to the Commons that Churchill returned. At one bound he was propelled into the new Cabinet. Baldwin offered and Churchill gladly accepted the post of Chancellor of the Exchequer. It was the least one Harrovian could do for another. A more likely explanation, however, was that when it became clear that Neville Chamberlain did not want to return to the Exchequer, Baldwin felt that it was better to have Churchill at the heart of his administration rather than skulking unpredictably on the back benches. It was a shrewd calculation, but many ordinary Conservatives, in the Commons and beyond, could not easily reconcile themselves to the central position in the government which the prodigal son had now achieved for himself. What manner of chameleon was this man? Politicians could change parties once with relative impunity, but it was rather reprehensible to make a habit of it.

It is easy, in retrospect, to discern in Churchill's course

since 1918 a steady and controlled progression back to his 'natural' home. The Liberal Party had outlived its usefulness and could never be put together again as a party of power. Given his previous defection, however, his re-entry had to be carefully negotiated so that it did not appear too blatantly self-seeking. The apparent failure of Conservative protectionism in 1923, coupled with the Socialist spectre, made the transition seem logical and acceptable. There was a new agenda in British politics and in the 'coming struggle for power' Churchill could only be on one side.

His instinct told him that sober bourgeois Europe – on which he relied as the necessary backdrop to his own exuberant aristocratic conduct – was grievously wounded by the necessary war of 1914–18, whose progress he continued to chronicle. Volume III grappled increasingly lugubriously with the slaughter of the Somme and Verdun. His instinct also told him that Socialism would not work and that the Soviet tyranny would be one of the worst in human history. The articulation of this sentiment in uncompromising language upset not only Socialists but academic and other observers who wanted to give the new civilisation a chance. Churchill's striking verbosity made it easy for them to dismiss him as 'reactionary'. In welcoming him back into the fold, some Conservatives remained suspicious that he was a wolf in penitent sheep's clothing. It appeared obvious that he loved the life of politics, that he yearned for high office – but was that all? He declaimed *against* Socialism but what was he *for*? Beneath the trappings of office was he one of the 'hollow men' identified by young Mr T.S. Eliot?

It was obvious that he did love the trappings of this particular office. He was able to wear the robes worn by his father. In addition, as Chancellor he could become the second most powerful man in the Cabinet, perhaps with right of succession, and thus at length realise prophecies made for a quarter of a century about his ultimate destiny. On the other hand, despite the administrative experience which he had built up over decades and the self-confidence in his own argumentative capacity which was part and parcel of that experience, Churchill could not claim deep personal knowledge in the realms of economics and finance. He would never confess himself to be out of his depth, but he might be. Of course, a profound grasp of these matters was not in itself a requirement of appointment. Even with the gaps in his knowledge, Winston started from a better position than Disraeli or even Lloyd George. Nevertheless, the complex financial aftermath of the war – reparations and war-debts – added immeasurably to the burdens of the Chancellor. One of the first things that Churchill noted on returning to high office was the burden of work with which he had to deal. His unusual methods and hours of conducting business were not only dictated by his peculiar metabolism. They reflected his need to let clever Treasury officials know that he had his own way of dealing with things, that he was and always would be a politician, even when dealing with issues of exquisitely technical character. His continuing insistence on drafting his own speeches and on injecting his own phrases into papers prepared by his officials was a sign of the same phenomenon. Such insertions were in large measure a waste of time; but that was the point in making them.

His language, on entering office, remained ambitious. He had himself supposed that he would be Minister of Health rather than Chancellor and had been immediately reaching into the recesses of memory for 'immense schemes' in the sphere of housing and other social services. He still regarded himself as progressive in these matters. Now that he was Chancellor, he could still talk about insurance and pensions. The Treasury, of course, had a traditional superintending function over expenditure in all departments and Churchill certainly saw no reason to detach himself from the intimate concerns of his colleagues. Inevitably, he met resistance, but it was sometimes more obdurate than he expected or liked. His political position was in fact only deceptively strong. He could not readily offend or oppose a Prime Minister who had so unexpectedly inserted him into the heart of a Cabinet some of whose members had eyed him with suspicion for decades. Both Austen and Neville Chamberlain, Foreign Secretary and Minister of Health respectively, were former Chancellors of the Exchequer. Churchill was a Free Trader surrounded by frustrated Protectionists. He dare not rock the boat if he seriously wished to persuade the Conservatives that he really had become a faithful party member. He was more beholden to the advice of experts than his manoeuvres suggested. He found it difficult to decide when experts disagreed because he did not have that intuition about figures which he thought he had about ships. What drove him, in the end, to a decision was a sense of the rightness of things drawn from spheres which did not derive directly from the financial world.

So it was with the single most important decision he took: to return to the Gold Standard at the pre-war parity of $4.86, announced in his budget on 28 April 1925. It was not a hasty or ill-considered outcome. The First World War had inevitably gravely disturbed the functioning of the international monetary system. An Act of 1919 had suspended the Gold Standard – the fixed price at which gold traded in the major world currencies – but only for six years. It remained a common article of faith, however, that the existence of such a Gold Standard was a vital ingredient in stabilising the international money markets and promoting international trade. Only a few commentators believed that the attempt to fix parities in terms of gold was either unneccessary or impossible. Churchill consulted widely and listened to conflicting opinion from economists and financial authorities. The decision to return to gold – though not, as it turned out, a return to minting gold coins – accorded with the belief that the time was ripe for the restoration of the pre-war trading and monetary system. Keynes shortly afterwards launched a formidable criticism under the title *The Economic Consequences of Mr Churchill*, but he was in a minority. At the time, it was generally conceived to be a bold and courageous step to take. There would be pain but it offered a path to progress.

Churchill's action has been as generally criticised in retrospect, as it was welcomed by contemporaries. Criticism has centred as much on the parity adopted as on the return to the Gold Standard itself. It has sometimes been suggested that Churchill himself was privately rather more unhappy than he appeared, but the evidence for this is not strong. Of course, technical arguments can and do continue, but whatever verdict on the precise decision is reached, it is clear that it was achieved within a 'City' rather than an 'industrial' context. Churchill himself was so remote, in his own personal links, from the world of industrial Britain that he was not able to supply the fresh perspective that might have been helpful. In every year that passed after the end of the war the problems of the so-called staple export industries became more acute as they grappled with changed market conditions. Churchill was not insensitive to these problems, but it was another matter to suggest how they might be solved. Nowhere, in the sphere of government, were the limitations of power more apparent.

Churchill vigorously asserted that the Gold Standard was no more responsible for the parlous condition of the coal industry – increased foreign competition, falling exports, inadequate machinery – than was the Gulf Stream. On the other hand, his action certainly did not improve matters and the problems of that industry were coming to a head. In the summer of 1925 he had supported the payment of a subsidy while a commission of enquiry investigated the industry's difficulties (and the government refined its plans for dealing with a possible strike). The report of the commission offered no short-term solution and tried to find a balance between the position of the owners and that of the miners: it rejected an increase in the hours of work but accepted that wages would have to fall.

The crisis came to a head in the early days of May 1926. Churchill's previous pre-war attitudes created the conviction in Labour and trade union circles that the Chancellor was the foremost 'hawk' in the Cabinet, anxious for a trial of strength. In fact, at least in relation to the challenge presented by the notion of a General Strike, there was little disagreement amongst colleagues. Churchill swelled the ministerial chorus that the issue had ceased to be about the wages of miners and had become whether the wishes of a democratically-elected government should be overthrown. Having put matters in those terms, Churchill's temperament, experience and philosophy of power required that he should go out and win the 'war'. As always, a crisis made him excited and energetic. His interventions were frequent and paid little attention to departmental boundaries, and he had no hesitation in telling the Home and War Secretaries what his experience suggested they should do. He wanted, and obtained, a plan to use the Territorials, without rifles, as a police reserve. The main focus of his activities, however, was in the production of the *British Gazette*, a government newspaper which purported to be 'an authoritative journal' but which, naturally enough, presented the dispute as one in which 'the nation' was being attacked by an 'enemy' with whom there could be no compromise. That perception led Churchill likewise to seek to put pressure on the new BBC to be as much an expression of the government's position as the *British Gazette*, but while not unsympathetic, John Reith, the Managing Director, refused to accept that degree of subordination.

Churchill's conduct during the General Strike naturally earned him praise and criticism – in different quarters. The *New Statesman* alleged that Churchill had remarked that 'a little blood-letting' would be all to the good – a remark he vehemently denied. However, both opponents and admirers regarded him, for good or ill, as the man whose language and attitudes raised the temperature of the dispute. The excitable Churchill was compared to his disadvantage with the emollient Baldwin. It was noted that revolutionary fervour was not conspicuous amongst the members of the TUC General Council and that, for the most part, the course of the strike was not marred by serious incidents of violence.

The contrast between the supposed positions of individual members of the Cabinet, however, can be overdrawn. There was a necessary part, in the government's strategy, both for belligerent figures and for conciliatory figures. Churchill's stance, however congenial it was to him, was not the wild and wayward course of a minister who had lost his head. It was one aspect of a multi-faceted strategy which aimed to produce 'victory'. Baldwin's claim that he was 'frightened' of what Churchill might do has to be seen in this context. And indeed, after the general strike ended, Churchill had no wish to prolong the miners' strike and took a prominent and relatively conciliatory role. Tom Jones recorded in his diary that Churchill was prepared to reach a settlement on hours, wages and conditions which terrified his colleagues and which they did not accept.[5] In his mind, there was no contradiction in his behaviour. A General Strike was a General Strike, even if those who took part in it did not envisage themselves as taking a course of action which challenged the authority of the State. It was a matter of power. It was necessary to show that government could not be coerced by such a tactic. Churchill did not mind if on such an issue he were typecast.

The return to the Gold Standard and the General Strike are the two aspects of Churchill's tenure of the Exchequer which are most frequently noted. Churchill himself, however, neither at the time nor subsequently, wished to encourage such a concentration of attention. He devoted a great deal of time to the presentation of his successive Budgets and finan-

cial statements. They rated highly as parliamentary performances but, despite the ingenuity he displayed, the overall
impact was disappointing, not least to Churchill himself. A
betting tax, for example, conspicuously backfired. He could
claim some credit for improvements in insurance and pensions
provision but in these areas he was apt to exaggerate his own
contribution at the expense of Neville Chamberlain, who was
proving a very active Minister of Health. His initial reduction
in Income Tax was designed to be both 'fair' and a stimulus
to enterprise. His later enthusiasm for a comprehensive
scheme of de-rating as a stimulus to economic recovery was a
characteristically 'big idea' which proved more complex to
introduce than he had anticipated, and was in any event not
likely to yield quite the reward which he expected. Financial
orthodoxy required that he should make reductions in
expenditure elsewhere to pay for these changes.

He was bold enough, therefore, to say in his first Budget
that he aimed to make substantial savings in the Service
Estimates. In this respect, he was poacher turned game-
keeper, and pressed the Admiralty hard to reduce its planned
expenditure. He found himself faced at one point with the
possible resignation of the entire Admiralty Board. He also
had to hold back the RAF which only a few years earlier he
had been responsible for developing. He showed a similar
scepticism about the development of a new naval base at
Singapore which he had previously supported. Clearly, he
was finding it very difficult to balance his immediate financial
priorities, made worse by the impact of the General Strike on
revenues, with his own fundamental assumptions about the
role of power in relations between states. This time the
exigencies of his present office required him to temper those
assumptions.

In this context, he found reasons to look upon world
developments with a mild optimism. The League of Nations,
at the time of its inauguration in 1919 and for some years
after, had not been the kind of organisation to appeal to
someone with Churchill's assumptions about power. By 1924,
however, he was writing that it was 'the duty of all' to sustain
and aid the League of Nations. In his arguments with the
various services Churchill continued to adhere to the philosophy underlying the 'Ten Year Rule' – that there would be
no war for ten years, a date, moreover, which constantly

moved forward. He supported it, for example, against Balfour in June 1928 when its premise was thoroughly debated. Churchill declared that 'there was no likelihood of a great war, and there was therefore no need for us to be in the state of instant readiness which was found necessary in the years prior to 1914'.[6] The Committee of Imperial Defence therefore agreed to maintain the ten-year horizon, subject to an annual reconsideration.

More specifically, 'appeasement' seemed to be working in Europe and the Locarno agreements, negotiated by the Foreign Secretary in August 1925, suggested the possibility of comprehensive reconciliation. Not that Churchill saw these treaties of mutual guarantee between the major European powers (the Soviet Union apart) as the prelude to a closer involvement in European affairs or in plans, to be unveiled a few years later by the French statesman, Aristide Briand, for closer European integration. On the contrary, Churchill belonged to that section of the Cabinet which welcomed Locarno precisely in the extent to which the improved Franco-German relationship enabled Britain to remained detached from Europe and able to concentrate on more important matters. Since Churchill was also firmly assuring Baldwin that there was not 'the slightest chance' of war with Japan in their lifetime, the auguries for lasting international peace did indeed appear promising. Churchill continued to see the Soviet state as a menace and was amongst that group which pressed for the breaking off of diplomatic relations in 1927.

Nobody supposed, in short, that Churchill had become overnight a pacifist, to use a word which had gained currency. When Lord Cecil, the League of Nations and disarmament enthusiast, finally resigned from the government in 1927, he singled out for special condemnation what he regarded as Churchill's attitude towards arms limitation at the Naval Disarmament Conference in Geneva. Churchill also made it clear, for example, that he supported the despatch of British forces to Shanghai in 1927, where British lives and property were being threatened.

> Short of being actually conquered [he wrote] there is no evil worse than submitting to wrong and violence for fear of war. Once you take the position of not being able in any circumstances to defend your rights against the aggression of some particular

set of people, there is no end to the demands that will be made or to the humiliations that must be accepted.[7]

Throughout his years as Chancellor of the Exchequer, his physical presence, distinctive speech and resounding rhetoric kept him in the public eye. Some of his speeches were brilliant, as Baldwin was forced to admit, though he did not like using the word because it reminded him of brilliantine, a substance he disliked. When Cabinet colleagues exchanged notes, they normally conceded that his good points outweighed his bad ones. Neville Chamberlain, however, sympathised with anyone on Churchill's personal staff who had to deal with so mercurial a master.

There were less sympathetic remarks about the company Churchill kept. Now that the Chartwell house was fully operational, Winston entertained in lavish style, that is to say often provided unlimited champagne, cigars and brandy. The host did not refrain from consuming in generous measure. He was emphatically a figure 'larger than life'. He had completed the fourth volume of *The World Crisis* while in office and was now engaged on a final volume which would consider *The Aftermath*. In addition, he could now lay two hundred bricks a day – a modest accomplishment, but not widespread amongst ministers. He still painted. These diverse achievements were not readily found elsewhere, least of all in the Cabinet. Yet this prodigious talent still seemed undisciplined and unpredictable. Churchill might go the way of his old friend F.E. Smith, whose fitfully brilliant legal and political career had fizzled out and who was now near the end of his life. If anything, as Winston grew older, he became even less inclined to seek out the company of those who might be regarded as equals. He liked to hold court rather than participate in a colloquium. Odd professors, like the Oxford physicist F.A. Lindemann, came to him; he did not go to universities.[8] A rather calculated disreputability surrounded a Chancellor of undoubted probity.

Somehow, the parts remained better than the sum. It was a verdict, too, which might be made on his tenure of the Exchequer. It did not quite add up to a convincing whole, though to suggest that he was a very bad Chancellor is to take too narrowly economic a conception of his function. As the span of the government drew to a close in 1928/9 he could undoubtedly be regarded as one of its successes. There was inevitably speculation about where to put him in the next administration. There was a case, Amery suggested to Neville Chamberlain, for making him Foreign Secretary. Chamberlain thought that such a prospect would cause the Prime Minister to wake up at nights with a cold sweat. There was a case, however, insofar as it was now the only major government post which Winston had never occupied. The somewhat disjointed reflections on foreign affairs which he had offered as Chancellor, in the margins, as it were, might become more rounded and coherent if he was forced departmentally to give himself to the systematic consideration of foreign affairs. Another thought was that he might become Lord President with special responsibility for the co-ordination of the services. Behind such reflections lay concern about the succession to Baldwin, whenever that might be. Although he was generally believed to have behaved well, a substantial number of Tories could not feel comfortable that a man with Churchill's record could be their leader and Prime Minister. Neville Chamberlain should be first lieutenant and heir-apparent. Perhaps the answer was to make Churchill Secretary of State for India?

All such speculation was based on the assumption that the Tories would form the next government. Although Churchill mocked some of the suggestions now made by Lloyd George to conquer unemployment, he could without much difficulty have adopted them himself. The Liberal challenge appeared unexpectedly strong, casting doubt on the assumption that the political struggle was 'anti-Socialist'. Churchill played an active part in the campaign for the election which was held on 30 May, but was not sanguine about the outcome. Not for him a Baldwinian emphasis on 'Safety First'. He preferred a robust onslaught on the perils of Socialism. In the event, although he succeeded in holding his own seat, albeit on a minority of the total poll, the scale of Conservative losses exceeded his expectations. His ejaculations to the surrounding staff in 10 Downing Street as the results came through were unprintable. He might have served in a Cabinet for the last time.

A POWERLESS DECADE: 1929–39

It had been noted that a period of sustained parliamentary
Opposition had never featured in Churchill's understanding
of political life. He had normally spent the relatively few years
in which he was not in office changing parties rather than
seeking to undermine governments. It was difficult to believe
that at the age of fifty four he would develop a new passion
for a 'shadow' role. The incoming Labour government looked
more secure than its predecessor and Winston would be in his
late fifties at the anticipated time of the next election. 'Only
one goal still attracts me', he wrote to his wife on 27 August
1929, '& if that were barred I shd quit the dreary field for
pastures new.'[9] It must be presumed that he was referring to
the leadership of the Conservative Party, and the prospect of
the premiership, since in the previous sentence he declared
that if Neville Chamberlain became party leader, 'or anyone
else of that kind', he would clear out of politics altogether and
concentrate on improving his fortune for the benefit of his
family. Chamberlain was five years older than Churchill.
Even so, supposing he did succeed Baldwin, Winston would
probably be too old to succeed him – in perhaps a decade.
On the other hand, the relative paucity of experienced talent
in the next generation might give the old men an additional
period of power. Churchill had sufficient experience of the
vicissitudes of politics to realise the fragility of such calcula-
tions but when there was 'only one goal left' he had to be
realistic about his chances.

In the event, Neville Chamberlain did succeed Baldwin but
at a date and after a set of developments which were not
anticipated by the leading Conservative actors in 1929. There
was to be no place for Churchill either in the National
Government formed by Ramsay MacDonald in 1931 or in the
National Government formed by Baldwin in 1935 or in the
National Government formed by Chamberlain in 1937. The
outcomes, in each case, might have been different if Churchill
had played his cards differently in the immediately anteceding
years. He still had a kind of power throughout this decade,
even though it did not derive from the possession of office. He
had the prestige which accrued from a career of extraordinary

variety and vigour. Here was a man, despite his flaws, who was 'waiting in the wings'. He had the power of the pen to a degree rare among his peers. He could still reach a readership at home and abroad through his sustained journalism on miscellaneous topics. He was a 'name' to hundreds of thousands of readers who neither knew nor cared whether he was an assiduous member of parliament. He had the power of speech, which could still be devastating, but was perhaps not so well-attuned to the more prosaic atmosphere of a Britain inhabited by radio listeners. His mode of expression, in whatever medium he used, excited admiration even if his sentiments did not. From his point of view, therefore, there was an acute danger that his cadences had lost their power to persuade and convince – interesting survivals from a more spacious age. Indeed, was not Churchill himself, and all he stood for, an interesting museum piece, no longer of relevance to the politics of the thirties but certainly worth inspecting in his glass case?

The decade was a fascinating and frustrating one for Churchill himself because he half-believed that this was the case. Aspects of his behaviour suggested that he rather liked being an antique, flaunting his prejudices and indifferent to the impression they created. All the world was out of step except our Winnie. Surrounded by a motley band of acolytes, who fed his self-esteem and drank his whisky, he raised two fingers to the world (in what was not yet a victory sign) and disappeared into his study to dictate yet more books about himself and his famous ancestor, John, Duke of Marlborough – to the point that it was hard to tell which was which! He gave up playing polo at the age of fifty but he could still shoot. Politically, he sprayed his shots around in a manner which seemed increasingly reckless and futile. They were the actions of a man who had lost power and did not seriously expect to regain it. On the other hand, in the scattered profusion of his efforts, he might yet unexpectedly hit a vulnerable target and return triumphant to the top.

Politics, at his age, was like that. Contemporaries found it increasingly difficult to determine the balance in the maturing Churchill between deep conviction, tawdry prejudice, rampant ambition, magnanimous wisdom, puckish playfulness and wilful obstruction. Perhaps Churchill himself was not sure about that balance any longer, if he had ever been. He amused, amazed and angered in almost equal measure. His misfortune, it began to seem, was that he was too talented in too many directions. He was bored by the single-minded cultivation of smaller patches which apparently satisfied lesser men. 'So long as you are with us', wrote the historian G.M. Trevelyan from Cambridge, 'it cannot be said that the race of statesmen who are men of letters is extinct.'[10] Churchill was not extinct, but it was a little uncomfortable being a dying breed.

Churchill certainly set about consolidating his literary reputation with relish. Within a fortnight of leaving office, he set to work on the biography of the first Duke of Marlborough. A research assistant was installed and a rigorous production schedule established.[11] This was not the only project, however. At this juncture Churchill collected contracts with the assiduity his revered monarch devoted to the collection of postage stamps. Besides magazine articles, he had two other substantial projects on the stocks – a final volume of *The World Crisis* which would deal with the Eastern Front in the early years of the war, and the volume of memoirs which were to appear under the title *My Early Life*. His income from literary activities was in the region of £30,000 a year at this time and far exceeded that from investments and his parliamentary salary. When a substantial amount of this income was invested it would give Churchill the financial security which his status, aspirations and activities required, but which he had never really possessed. Literary fame and financial well-being thus blended conveniently.

The production schedule was relentlessly adhered to. It was given fresh urgency by the fact that the investment income looked forward to in the summer of 1929 suffered severely as a result of the Great Crash in the United States in the following October. Serialised in advance in, or reprinted from, one newspaper or another, the following books kept Churchill in the headlines. *My Early Life* (1930) covered the years from his birth to the death of Queen Victoria in 1901. 'You are an interesting cuss', said the Prime Minister, Ramsay MacDonald, in thanking Winston for sending him a copy.[12] Many readers agreed. The early man revealed was sentimental and pugnacious but curiously without guile and almost defenceless. A politician who reveals that much about himself has either abandoned the pursuit of power or is consciously inviting a public, upon whom he might yet depend for support, to see in this self-revelation a full, if flawed, human being. Neville Chamberlain would never take the public into his confidence to such an extent. The other two volumes, *Thoughts and Adventures* (1932) and *Great Contemporaries* (1937) were less personally self-revelatory but the former, a selection of his myriad articles, provides glimpses of his assumptions and concerns at this time. These were not academic treatises but crafted contributions for a wide audience for a fee. He wrote about topics on which he was knowledgeable and about which he knew little with apparently equal fluency.

Two themes emerge from these books and surrounding miscellaneous correspondence, articles and comments: the loss of power and the inhospitableness of the future. It was inevitable that reflection on his early life should lead him to compare it with the early 1930s. He realised, as he wrote in his famous preface, that he had drawn a picture of a vanished age. He was a child of the Victorian era when Britain's position in trade and on the seas was 'unrivalled'. The greatness of the Empire and the duty to preserve it was axiomatic. The 'dominant forces' at home were sure of themselves and of their doctrines. Supremacy at sea[13] brought them security and the confidence that they could teach the world the art of government and the science of economics. They rested 'sedately under the convictions of power'. They did so no longer. The island had indeed fallen into a 'rotten state'.

Part of the problem now was to identify those 'dominant forces'. Where did power actually lie? The funeral of his cousin, the ninth Duke of Marlborough, in 1934, occasioned poignant and puzzled reflections. Three or four hundred families, he supposed, had given Britain its political leadership during the centuries which had witnessed its emergence as a Great Power. They were now almost entirely powerless and with the politics of privilege had gone the politics of intellect. As Cowling points out, this was in part a mere reiteration of the resentment of the 'first-class brains' for the 'race of pygmies' who had come into office after 1922.[14] However much he himself belonged to one of these families, he did not object to the arrival of a kind of democracy but he wondered how much benefit there was in the apparent replacement of an ancient political aristocracy by self-made millionaires, pugilists and film-stars. Mass society had an education which was at once universal and superficial (it devoured his articles!).

How could political power be exercised in such conditions? He could not quite accommodate himself to the fact that a minister was 'no longer a figure of mystery and awe'. He was now expected to wear 'plus fours' and wait his turn on the links like any man. Could leadership arise from 'ordinary fellows' who just happened to have a peculiar kind of large-scale work to do? He assumed that the handling of power required a man 'to be uplifted above the general mass', as he was himself. But was this necessarily so? What if the unmasking of the mystery of power revealed that there was no mystery after all? Churchill could not really believe that. Indeed, looking around at the demise almost everywhere of that vague and mild Liberalism in which he himself had believed earlier in the century, he saw not the emergence of 'ordinary fellows' capably running complex modern states but rather 'a violent reaction against Parliamentary and electioneering procedure' and 'the establishment of dictatorships real or veiled in almost every country'. He could indeed see why a Mussolini had emerged in Italy – 'the greatest lawgiver among living men' – but Fascism was no more the solution to Britain's difficulties than was Communism. It was both desirable and possible to preserve a parliamentary system of government 'with whatever modifications may be necessary'. One suggestion he made, perhaps arising out of his own experience at the Treasury, was the impractical one of putting all matters economic in the hands of a specialist Economic Council which could determine policy free from the electoral considerations which disfigured proper policy formulation in parliament. He liked, too, to see in himself a specimen of the singular British capacity to manage political change in such a way that bright stars who shone under one dispensation could continue to do so in very different political circumstances. The only difficulty with this reflection was that he did not appear to be shining very brightly at this particular juncture when, he increasingly believed, the survival of the country was at stake.

It was not only because of the tensions arising out of the transition to mass politics that Churchill felt apprehensive about the future. His early general enthusiasm for 'science' and its beneficial possibilities had been increasingly replaced by alarm at what it meant in practice. The remarkable Professor Lindemann, who needed neither wine nor meat to enable him to have profound scientific thoughts, appealed to Churchill because of his facility in explaining the implications of various scientific discoveries. Churchill's enthusiasm for new machines was undimmed, but the more he heard from 'The Prof' and the more he observed the conformity and standardisation which 'science' required, the more gloomy he became. 'Science' was undermining the laws, customs, beliefs and instincts of mankind at an alarming rate. Of course, 'science' still had its good side but its awesome power to destroy could not be overlooked.

In these rather gloomy circumstances, there was only the past to turn to and the life of *Marlborough* which appeared in four volumes from 1933 to 1938 suited the purpose admirably. Churchill was serious, had his documents prepared properly for his attention and talked to and corresponded with academic specialists. He felt he had an edge over academic specialists who only worked from documents because his own experience, which could reasonably be carried backwards, told him that a great many decisions were reached in government without leaving behind a recorded dossier. His zeal for authenticity took him to the battlefields to see for himself. 'I am now living in the wars of Marlborough', he wrote in January 1934 with scarcely any exaggeration.

Of course, *Marlborough* was a committed book and Churchill sought to exonerate his hero wherever he could. He was stirred by British armies on the continent of Europe and the constitutional freedoms which he believed they left behind them. The interplay between past and present was inescapable. Was this or that action inspired by Robert Harley or Stanley Baldwin? Historical analogy was always at the ready involving the name of Marlborough. For Louis XIV read Hitler. No other contemporary statesman in the world lived in such a constant dialogue with the past. The problem of power was all-pervasive. Indeed, in one of the *Marlborough* volumes Churchill felt obliged to write a purple passage in which he praised the legitimacy of the pursuit of power. He saw a distinction, however, between a Napoleon and a Marlborough, writing in 1934, 'Napoleon could order, but

Marlborough could never do more than persuade or cajole. It is hard to win battles on that basis.'[15] It was hard, too, for Churchill to win political battles in the 1930s on that basis.

Churchill's failure to be a 'man of power' during this decade stemmed from the fact that most of his political contemporaries had abandoned, or never held, his twin assumptions about the way British power could be sustained internationally and how political power could be exercised domestically in the electorate of the 1930s. Winston, wrote Irwin to Baldwin from the Viceregal Lodge in New Delhi in March 1929, 'has become – or perhaps it's more true to say – has always been, a much more vigorous Imperialist in the 1890–1900 sense of the word than you & me'.[16] Indeed, between 1929 and 1935, when the Government of India Act was eventually passed, Churchill seemed to have 'India on the brain'. His praise of the British record was not unreasonable. His alarm about the integrity of India and about the relationships between its people was not unfounded. He still believed that it was right *and feasible* to use 'our undoubted power' for the welfare of Indians and Britain alike. The Conservative leadership might like to have done so, but saw themselves being dragged into an unending conflict unless Indians were brought to a share of central government. No doubt full self-government lay somewhere further along the road.

Churchill was appalled at the prospect of the brightest jewel in the crown of the King being cast away merely because of the antics of Gandhi, the half-naked fakir who had the temerity to stride up the steps of the Viceregal palace. Winston's vision was apocalyptic. The loss of Britain's external connections would bring the 'surplus' population of Britain within measurable distance of utter ruin. He told Lord Linlithgow, who was to become Viceroy of India two years later, in an angry exchange of letters in May 1934, that England was now beginning a new period of struggle and fighting for its life.[17] The retention of India was one crucial element in survival. Linlithgow told him that he was spluttering 'the atavistic shibboleths of an age destined very soon to retreat into the forgotten past'.

Churchill's protracted campaign was a failure. He had resigned from the Shadow Cabinet in January 1931 and may have supposed that he could use the Indian issue to topple

Baldwin from the leadership of the Conservative Party. If so, he was disappointed. He was never to attract more than a relatively small band of 'die-hards', and embarrassed some of his younger admirers by choosing this particular issue on which to make a challenge. Although Churchill claimed that it was Baldwin who was dividing the party, insofar as he was departing from its 'historic' attitudes on Egypt, India and the Empire generally, that was not how matters seemed to most Conservative MPs. His opponents were not averse to a certain chicanery in helping the Government of India Bill on its way, but the attitude Churchill displayed throughout the struggle alienated rather than attracted support. In the circumstances, there had been no invitation to join MacDonald's National Government in 1931 and Baldwin saw no reason to extend an olive branch and include him in the administration he formed in 1935. Overall, Winston had diminished rather than enhanced his credibility and stature. Indeed, more than that, his behaviour in opposing the party leadership confirmed, yet again, to many Conservative MPs that he could not understand the meaning of party loyalty. He was a spent force. Men who dismissed him for this reason were not disposed to take him seriously when he now began to talk about Europe.

Churchill's view of the world in the middle 1930s suggested that within the space of six years it had become a very dangerous place. He still seemed to believe, however, that Britain's 'undoubted power' could be deployed universally. Yet could it? He could see that there was a problem of will, without which even the possession of the most formidable forces was pointless. In September 1930 he expressed his bewilderment to Beaverbrook. How was it that the same people who had poured out blood and money to hold Ypres 'should now throw away our conquests and our inheritance with both hands, through helplessness and pusillanimity'? He could not grasp the extent to which the experience of the Great War made millions unwilling to face another, except when it became apparent beyond doubt that there was no alternative. Neither could he appreciate that a younger generation, at least, felt awkward about taking pride in the mere fact of 'conquest'. Churchill declared that his only interest in politics was to retrieve a situation in which 'the miserable public' even took it as an open question whether Britain should not clear out of India altogether. If he told 'the people' 'the truth' then surely all would be well? It was a quixotic enterprise which, on the terms he desired, could not succeed.[18]

Baldwin understood that 'the miserable public' was not so easily convinced. He was not a man of Empire in his bones. He had no war memoirs to write. The world of 1914 had passed away. A Prime Minister was not controlled by a League of Nations Union or paralysed by a Peace Ballot, but he had to be elected. He felt certain that if he had gone to the country in 1935 with a publicised programme of substantial rearmament he would have lost. People would only 'sit up' when they thought that the dictators might attack them. A democratic government could not do more than 'persuade or cajole', to use Churchill's words of Marlborough, and make whatever preparations it could within a framework which the people were prepared to accept. Baldwin's concept of the relationship between Prime Minister and people was fortified by his deft handling of the Abdication crisis. He was on the right wavelength whilst Churchill romantically but futilely stood by Edward VIII.[19]

A man who is not in power, however, can be a Cassandra. After 1932 Churchill certainly identified the threat which a rearmed Germany would pose to the stability of Europe, an anxiety which deepened after the advent of Hitler to power. Precisely what should be done, however, was not clear. The most passionate exchanges with government ministers concerned both the potential and levels of air power in Britain and in Germany. It was difficult for contemporaries to determine where the truth lay and has not been easy for subsequent historians. Churchill was indeed drawn 'inside' by accepting membership of the sub-committee on Air Defence Research. *Marlborough* and India meant that his attention was by no means concentrated single-mindedly on European developments. He was prudently out of the country at critical moments, for example at the time of the revelation of the Hoare-Laval pact concerning the future of Abyssinia.

Since he did not need to make decisions, his warnings through the mid-thirties could continue at a high level of generality, and avoid certain awkward topics altogether. Indeed, as the Baldwin government came to an end, there was a sense in which he was 'half-in and half-out', particularly in respect to air matters. He agreed to second a motion nominating Chamberlain as Leader of the Conservative Party in May 1937 and had hopes that he might be invited to join the new Cabinet.[20] Although this was not forthcoming, Churchill seemed to be mending bridges. He confined his criticisms almost exclusively to private correspondence for the rest of 1937. He did not become Minister for the Coordination of Defence. All the while, however, he continued to build up, through private and some official channels, a vast reservoir of miscellaneous information against the day when it might be needed.

Other moves he made at this juncture displayed a pragmatism which some observers found surprising. From 1936 onwards, he came more and more into association with certain Liberal and Labour politicians. In the past they had regarded him as incurably 'reactionary' but now found him enthusiastic for the League of Nations and unexpectedly eager to draw the Soviet Union into a 'grand alliance'. It was indeed the case that his identification of Germany as the main immediate threat to the peace of Europe led him to subordinate his hostility to Communism. He also expressed the hope that the United States might be drawn into taking a more active interest in European problems. It was perhaps no accident that his latest literary project was to be *A History of the English-Speaking Peoples*. The lecture tours which he had undertaken in North America had not only been good for his purse. They gave him a sense of self-importance at a time when he no longer seemed a man of power. In Canada, for example, he talked enthusiastically about the depth of imperial ties – something which 'the Europeans' could never understand. He talked to Americans about common ideals. There was safety in such generalities. In private, however, he felt some ambivalence about the United States. In the late 1920s, he took strong exception to what he took to be the American bid for naval supremacy. In October 1937 he wrote privately that while the ideals of Britain and America were similar, their interests were in many ways divergent.[21]

That distinction was very relevant to the deteriorating situation in Europe. Churchill issued solemn warnings to the government. The visit of Lord Halifax to Germany in November 1937 led Winston in the Commons to warn against the folly of making terms for Britain at the expense either of small nations or large ideals. His premonitions of impending disaster strengthened after Eden's resignation as Foreign Secretary in February 1938. He chose to interpret Eden's action as that of a strong young figure standing out against 'long, dismal, drawling tides of Drift and surrender'. The Austrian *Anschluss* of March 1938 was another indication that Europe was confronted with 'a programme of aggression, nicely calculated and timed'. Countries were increasingly being faced with a choice between submitting and taking 'effective measures' while time remained. For Churchill that meant talking about the 'reign of law in Europe' and bringing the small states of the continent together. He continued to press the government on its rearmament programme in general and the question of air parity with Germany in particular. Britain and France had to stand together. He even went to Paris in person to stress this point to certain leading French politicians. It would be wrong, however, to believe that in these months Churchill did nothing but lobby and make speeches. He was still deeply immersed in his writing, both the final volume of *Marlborough* and the first chapter of his new work on *The English-Speaking Peoples*.

He surfaced, however, as the future of Czechoslovakia came into question, to reiterate his belief that Britain, France and Russia, acting in concert, could certainly prevent the disaster of war. He showed sympathy with the position of the 'Sudeten' Germans – of whom there were some three million living in Czechoslovakia when that country's boundaries had been settled at the end of the First World War – but believed that their 'leader', Konrad Henlein, whom he met, would accept 'autonomy'. Churchill opposed the transfer of the Sudetenland to Germany. In the days in late September, when Chamberlain was flying to and from Germany, Churchill watched events keenly, frightened that the Prime Minister would bring back 'peace with dishonour'. In the end, it seemed to him that the Munich Agreement was just such a settlement. He was contemptuous of those who believed that the pacification of Europe had been achieved. In the Commons he spoke in melancholy terms of the fate of Czechoslovakia. The country had suffered in every respect from her association with the western democracies. The Munich Agreement was 'a total and unmitigated defeat'. The people should know the truth. There had been a gross neglect and deficiency in Britain's defensive preparations. The whole equilibrium of Europe had been deranged. It was a message that most MPs and members of the public did not want to hear. He was a prophet without honour in his own country. The nation would pay a terrible price for its foolish failure to understand the logic of power.

The invasion of Prague in March 1939 was further confirmation for Churchill that his intuitive assessment of the political reality in Europe was correct. He kept up his pressure on the Prime Minister both with regard to the establishment of a Ministry of Supply and with respect to negotiations with Moscow. Throughout these anxious months, his life continued to consist of writing history and commenting on present politics. One of his associates, Brendan Bracken, wrote at the time that no public man had shown more foresight. His long and lonely struggle to expose the dangers of dictatorship would prove 'to be the best chapter in his crowded life'. In fact, there was to be another chapter, but in many respects that subsequent chapter was only made possible by his stand in these years. It may now appear, in the light of all we know about the complexities of the choices that had to be made by the British government, that Churchill oversimplified the issues. We may also feel that Churchill's own account of his views in *The Gathering Storm* exaggerates the clarity, consistency and continuity of his own position. The important fact, however, was that he came increasingly to be thought by public opinion to be more right than wrong in his view of Hitler and the measures that might have been taken to avoid the 'unnecessary war'. It had been frustrating not to be a man of power, but his lack of office was in fact his salvation. Personally, too, after all his isolation and depression, after his strong sense of impending old age, he felt suddenly young, alert and confident. Once again, the extraordinary vicissitudes of politics were revealed. He would go down in history as the man who stood out against 'appeasement' and, in the most perilous circumstances, he was back once more on the path to power.

· · ·

NOTES AND REFERENCES

1. Martin Gilbert, *Winston S. Churchill*, Volume IV, *1917–1922*, London, 1975, p. 891; W.M. Walker, 'Dundee's

Disenchantment with Churchill', *Scottish Historical Review*, xlix, 1970.

2. R. Prior, *Churchill's 'World Crisis' as History*, London, 1983.
3. M. Cowling, *Religion and Public Doctrine in Modern England*, Cambridge, 1980, p. 306.
4. Gilbert, *op.cit.*, p. 470.
5. K. Middlemas ed., *Thomas Jones: Whitehall Diary*, Volume ii, London, 1969, pp.56, 60–1.
6. Gilbert, *Winston S. Churchill*, Volume V, *1922–1939*, London, 1976, p. 290.
7. *Ibid*. p. 227.
8. He did, however, agree to become Chancellor of Bristol University in 1929.
9. Gilbert, *op.cit.*, p. 344.
10. *Ibid*. p. 365.
11. J.H. Plumb, 'Churchill' in *The Making of an Historian: The Collected Essays of J.H. Plumb*, Volume i, London, 1988, pp. 238–40.
12. Gilbert, *op.cit.*, p. 365.
13. Winston S. Churchill, *My Early Life*, London, 1941, pp. 9–10.
14. Cited and discussed in Cowling, *Religion and Public Doctrine*, p. 308.
15. Gilbert, *op.cit.*, p. 500.
16. Gilbert, *Winston S. Churchill*, Volume V, Companion, Part I, London, 1979, p. 1452.
17. Gilbert, *Churchill*, Volume V, p. 482.
18. *Ibid*. pp. 365–6.
19. P. Ziegler, *Edward VIII*, London, 1990, pp. 316–17.
20. M. Cowling, *The Impact of Hitler: British Politics and British Policy 1933–1940*, Cambridge, 1975, pp. 239–45.
21. The background to some of the issues involved can be studied in David Reynolds, *The Creation of the Anglo-American Alliance 1937–1941: A Study in Competitive Co-operation*, London, 1981, and James R. Leutze, *Bargaining for Supremacy: Anglo-American Naval Collaboration 1937–1941*, Chapel Hill, 1977.

Chapter 5

IN COMMAND OF WAR
1939–1945

. . . . . .

FIRST LORD OF THE ADMIRALTY 1939–1940

The Prime Minister, Neville Chamberlain, broadcast to the nation at 11.15 on the morning of 3 September 1939 that Britain was at war with Germany. Two days earlier, Churchill had been privately offered a position in the small War Cabinet which Chamberlain proposed to form in what might be a Coalition government if Labour and the Liberals agreed. In the interval, since he heard nothing further from the Prime Minister, Churchill was puzzled both about the government's last-minute intentions and about his own position. Having heard the broadcast, however, and having survived an air-raid warning, Churchill made his way to the House of Commons. In his speech he did not underestimate the gravity of the task but was sure that it was not beyond the strength of the British Empire and the French Republic. It was not a question of fighting 'for' Danzig or 'for' Poland but of 'fighting to save the whole world from the pestilence of Nazi tyranny and in defence of all that is most sacred to man'. A strong sense of calm had come over him. He was conscious of 'a kind of uplifted detachment from human and personal affairs'.[1]

After the debate, Chamberlain informed him that he had decided to have the Service Ministers in the War Cabinet. As a result he proposed to offer Churchill the post of First Lord of the Admiralty. That same evening he made his first appearance at the Admiralty, and the Fleet was sent the signal, 'Winston is back'. It was almost uncanny that after twenty-five years he should return to the same office at the start of another war.

The significance of Churchill's appointment should not be exaggerated. In the summer, some newspapers had started to agitate for his inclusion in the government, but before the actual outbreak of war Chamberlain could still ignore this campaign. Between 1 and 3 September some of Churchill's associates, Boothby in particular, overestimated their hero's position. They urged him not to accept Chamberlain's offer but rather to go to the Commons and destroy the Prime Minister there and then. However, quite apart from the obvious risk of exposing a major political rift at the beginning of a war, it was not clear that Churchill would succeed and he would have been widely criticised for his temerity in trying. The fact was that Chamberlain still led the Conservative Party. Neither Labour nor the Liberals had joined the government, something the Prime Minister did not appear greatly to regret. He had a majority in the Commons of around two hundred and his War Cabinet consisted of tried and trusted associates – the newcomer, Churchill, apart. Chamberlain was to have no difficulty, for example, in excluding Churchill from the meetings of the Anglo-French Supreme War Council until February 1940.

Winston's sporadic assaults on the government over the previous half a dozen years had been essentially personal. He had not gathered an ever-growing band of supporters behind him, indeed he had scarcely made the attempt. It is a measure of the extent to which Churchill was regarded as a 'has been' that 'dissidents' looked rather to the much younger Anthony Eden as a possible 'coming man'. And Eden had accepted the position of Dominions Secretary. It was Chamberlain who was still firmly in the position of power, or so it appeared. Leo Amery wrote in his diary that he expected Churchill to be Prime Minister before the end of the year, but there did not seem very strong grounds for such an opinion.

The longer-term fate of the government depended, once again, on contrasting conceptions of power. It was a commonplace that Neville Chamberlain, who was even older than Churchill, was not by temperament or inclination a 'natural war leader'. Quite apart from his awareness of the suffering war would bring, he had thought for at least a decade that an extended war would be likely to be catastrophic for the British

Empire. A war might begin in one continent but it would be unlikely to end there. As late as March 1939, Churchill was writing to him inviting him to 'consider how vain is the menace that Japan will send a fleet and army to conquer Singapore'.[2]

Chamberlain was not so sure. In effect, to use the language of one historian, the Prime Minister had come to sense that the British Empire survived not because it was an empire of power but because, after the initial assertion of British power, most of its inhabitants had fallen into the habit of accepting British authority. Japan did have real military power which could expose the limitations of British power and, *pace* Churchill, together with the obvious signs in India that 'authority' was no longer universally accepted, could bring about the total collapse of the Asian empire almost at a stroke.

The prospect of a war against Germany on the continent, against Italy in the Mediterranean and against Japan in East Asia had been for him a recurring nightmare, particularly since American support was unlikely, Dominion support grudging at best and Soviet support two-edged if available at all. His 'struggle for peace' and pursuit of 'appeasement' derived from such perceptions.[3] He had now declared war, but he still hoped that an economic blockade would exacerbate the internal economic crisis in Germany which his own advisers had long thought likely. His own carefully-phased rearmament, he liked to think, would prevent such an economic crisis in Britain. It would still be possible to 'beat' Hitler, though possibly not overthrow him unless the Germans did that themselves, in a manner and on terms which would prevent a major European war with all its attendant global risks.

Churchill's instincts told him that such a timorous and realistic appraisal of power invited disaster. It was an attitude of mind produced by that loss of the will to power which he had so gloomily detected in the British political elite, corrupted as it had been by inappropriate moral sensitivities. You had to be willing (though not necessarily able) to fight everywhere against all comers if you were going to fight somewhere effectively against a particular opponent. Power could not be distributed or withheld by a British government in penny packets across the globe. Churchill did not quite know why wars came, but come they did. His study of history, his experience of the Great War and his inner disposition told him that wars could not be fought or won half-heartedly. The British Empire was more likely to be saved by vigorous imprudence in word and deed than by any other means.

It was this sense which was immediately communicated at the Admiralty, but it was an uncomfortable one. It was difficult to avoid the sensation of history repeating itself and for Admirals and their First Lord to be natural in their relations with each other and to banish or refresh, as appropriate, their collective memories of the controversies, structures and methods of the previous war. Churchill had then been a young man, bullying and brow-beating, on occasion, serving officers who were older than himself. Now he was older than they were and, while no less given to peremptory behaviour, was less abrasive. They in turn tended to be better educated and more articulate. Pound, the First Sea Lord, was not a Jackie Fisher. However, absence from this particular office and lengthy scrutiny of 1914/15 had not caused Churchill to modify his conception of his role. He probed and pressed at every point. He fairly and unfairly dismissed officers who displeased him. He searched for a naval offensive and Admirals trembled at the prospect of a Baltic adventure. Air and submarine power caused alarm, but not sufficient alarm. There was the excitement of the scuttling of the *Graf Spee* off Montevideo and the (illegal) capture of the *Altmark* in Norwegian waters. On the other hand, the *Royal Oak* had been sunk in Scapa Flow. These, and other episodes, combined to give Churchill and the navy special prominence in what was otherwise a 'phoney war'. It led to him being made chairman of the Military Coordination Committee, in addition to his other duties.

It was in both of these capacities, therefore, that Churchill had overall responsibility for British operations in Scandinavia in April 1940. A debatable British mine-laying operation off the Norwegian coast was overtaken, a few days later, by the German invasion of Denmark and Norway. The British reaction, while not without moments of inspiration, proved a disaster, conventionally attributed to bad intelligence and poor planning. The navy came face to face with the fact that control of the air was the vital factor in combined operations. The assumption, shared by Churchill, that Norway could not be successfully invaded by Germany while the British Navy was relatively close at hand at Scapa Flow, had been shattered. Needless to say, the extent to which the First Lord can be personally held responsible for the muddle in organisation and for the changes of plan, remains contentious. Churchill himself was scathing about the way in which decisions were made in the Military Coordination Committee. However, much criticism centres upon the Admiralty in particular, and Churchill cannot be completely exonerated. On the other hand, it is becoming clear that the information which Churchill had from Enigma cyphers was so dazzlingly complete and so new as a 'problem' that no one quite knew how to handle it operationally.[4]

The irony was that the fiasco in the North Sea brought Churchill to 10 Downing Street. The Prime Minister had been foolish enough to remark on the eve of his successful Scandinavian campaign that Hitler had 'missed the bus'. Now opinion in parliament and the country began seriously to fear the prospect of defeat. The discontent found open expression in the 'Norway Debate' of 7/8 May 1940. As he had to, Churchill spoke in defence both of the government and of himself, but the venom of the attack on him reluctantly persuaded Chamberlain that he had to stand down. It was the odd outcome of a division in which he still had a majority of 81 votes.

It was by no means self-evident, however, that Churchill was the only conceivable successor. Some, with whatever mixture of motives, hankered after the 77-year-old Lloyd George. The favourite was Lord Halifax, the Foreign Secretary, both in the eyes of Chamberlainites and of Labour – the man with whom (as Lord Irwin) Churchill had tangled over India. There is little doubt that Halifax could have become Prime Minister if he had wanted to. He no doubt sensed that he was no better equipped with belligerent qualities than Chamberlain. Even if he did become Prime Minister, Churchill would have to be Minister of Defence and would, in effect, be running the war. It was better, in these circumstances, that he should take over completely. On his own account, at his interview with Chamberlain, Halifax and Margesson, the Chief Whip, he kept unusually quiet. The result of this interview was an invitation from the king to form a government – which he eagerly accepted. He was Prime Minister at last.[5]

THE POWER OF THE PRIME MINISTER 1940–1945

i. Prime Ministers, Parties and Parliament

Churchill himself grandiloquently described all his past life
as a preparation for what now lay ahead of him. Indeed, no
other Prime Minister in the twentieth century, and few before
then, had reached the highest position in the land with so
wide a range of experience and attributes. The manner in
which he would wield power as Prime Minister would reflect
that prodigious diversity. For the first time, he would have
the ultimate power of decision. He had been irrepressible in
bombarding Prime Ministers, from Campbell-Bannerman to
Neville Chamberlain, with memoranda and suggestions that
went beyond his own immediate departmental responsibilities. They had their own ways of listening to or ignoring that
advice. Now he only had a dialogue with himself. It was
inconceivable that he would not continue to be fertile with
suggestions to colleagues but for the first time he could no
longer rely on someone else. In the past, often to his own
irritation at the time, another person had weeded out the
sense from the nonsense in his proposals. On the other hand,
he brought to his new office a matchless knowledge of how
other Prime Ministers had behaved, not least of the way in
which they had controlled him.[6]

The circumstances of his advent to power, although only
briefly described, are of fundamental importance. He had
come into contention because a Prime Minister had lost the
confidence of a substantial section of his own party. Formally
speaking, that Prime Minister had not lost the power to
govern. Chamberlain could have continued until he had been
defeated in the Commons. He could probably not have gone
on for very long, though there is no absolute certainty about
that. He chose to stand down rather than struggle on. It
followed that Churchill himself could fall from power in
comparable fashion. His position, therefore, was quite unlike
the other major figures of the war: Hitler, Stalin, Roosevelt.
They could be removed only by death from natural causes or
by assassination. Only Churchill could be removed by a vote
of a parliament if there was dissatisfaction with the conduct
of the war. Roosevelt, of course, had to submit himself for

election, but once elected, he was there for a fixed term. A President's power was not unlimited but it was more permanent. In international dealings through the war, therefore, the British Prime Minister could be more vulnerable than his counterparts.

In such company, a British Prime Minister would always have been in this position but Churchill's position was peculiar even so. Prime Ministers normally become Prime Ministers because they are leaders of parties, either of a party with an absolute majority in the Commons or with sufficient indication of support from another party to provide a majority. Churchill was not the leader of a party. On becoming Prime Minister, at the invitation of the Crown, he had not become party leader. Neville Chamberlain retained that position and was to do so until he died later in 1940. It is interesting to speculate on what might have happened in May 1940 if the *de facto* selection of a Prime Minister had taken place in a far wider circle than was in fact the case and had even involved the kind of balloting that exists in the contemporary Conservative Party and has been used to remove one Prime Minister and select her successor. It is by no means clear that Churchill would have become Prime Minister in such circumstances. It is true that he did become Leader of the Conservative Party after Chamberlain's death but that was a shot-gun marriage. Churchill well knew that he did not owe his position in Downing Street to the hierarchy of the Conservative Party or to any of its organs. When they looked at his record overall, many Conservative MPs could not support him without reservation and he, in turn, regarded many of them with suspicion. In this respect, the cooperative role of Chamberlain, in the last months of his life, in buttressing Churchill within the Conservative Party was of considerable importance.

The position was of particular delicacy because one way in which Churchill from the beginning sought to boost his own position was to pick up the theme of his own powerlessness in the 1930s and extract as much credit as possible from the fact that he was not a 'guilty man'. It did not take him long to squeeze out 'tainted' politicians, however high or low their estate. Lord Halifax was eased out of the Foreign Office to the Washington Embassy, an important post to be sure, but not so important as the Foreign Office. Sir Samuel Hoare was lucky to find himself demoted to the Madrid Embassy. The 'purge' was discrete and for the most part not acrimonious, but the Chamberlainites knew they were on their way to the periphery of the war. Everybody knew, however, that the issue of the direction of the Great War had caused, or at least precipitated, a fatal split in the mighty Liberal Party. Given the odd circumstances of 1940, it was not difficult to envisage another split in the Conservative Party if Churchill's perform-ance, for whatever reason, failed to satisfy.

Churchill's elevation was a parliamentary coup in a parlia-ment elected in 1935. As in 1914, war had come in 1939 when politicians were looking to an imminent election. There was much speculation on what the outcome might be, speculation continued by subsequent historians. We can guess that Labour might have made some gains but not sufficient to have been able to form a government. An increased Labour representation as the result of an election, if one had been held, would have given the House a different tone. As it was, however, and as it would remain for the rest of the war, the Prime Minister had to deal with MPs elected in very different circumstances and in the increasingly distant past. Since the major parties had agreed to an electoral truce there would be no significant change in the balance of opinion. Again, we can only guess what electoral endorsement Churchill might have received if there had been an election in 1940. The Prime Minister did not have to face this challenge and discover whether he was indeed 'the people's Winnie'.

In all these circumstances, there was a certain irony in the stress placed upon parliament in the British presentation of what the war was all about. It was necessary in propaganda terms to contrast the way in which the Prime Minister directed the war, in and through parliament, with the power of the dictators, who were not restrained or guided by representative institutions. In practice, too, the exigencies of decision-making made it more and more unconvincing to think that the House of Commons in wartime had the power to initiate legislation or exercise close monitoring of the War Cabinet. Nevertheless, it was to the Commons, in secret or open session, that Churchill had to come, in moments of triumph, disaster or routine ordinariness. He had to submit to criticism on matters great or small, sometimes to his intense annoyance. He had to respond in ways that would reassure and inspire, even when he felt criticisms were unfair or unhelpful. It was a restraint on power which no other major war leader had to endure. Only in the first six months of 1942, following the fall of Singapore and Tobruk, was there even the prospect that parliamentary criticism would put Churchill's position in any jeopardy. The vote of no confidence that followed the debate on 1/2 July gave the government 475 votes and its critics 25.[7]

The fact that this low dissenting vote can be judged the high point of parliamentary opposition during the war was of course largely testimony to extent to which the Coalition which Churchill had formed in May 1940 had effectively gelled. It came at almost exactly the same point in the Second War as it had in the First. However, Churchill did not form his Coalition as an incumbent Prime Minister, reluctantly broadening the party base of his government. His Coalition was a coalition from the outset and its composition reflected his need not only to create a government of national unity through multi-party participation but to do so in a fashion which ensured his own personal power. The result was a strange mixture of 'Churchill's friends', non-party men and formal inter-party appointments. At the beginning, in a five-man War Cabinet, Churchill was joined by Chamberlain and Halifax, and Attlee and Greenwood from Labour. The three Service ministers – Alexander, Admiralty (Labour), Eden, War (Conservative) and Sinclair, Air (Liberal) – would not prove awkward. Lord Lloyd as Colonial Secretary could be relied on to have sound views on Empire. The breadth of opinion was further reflected in appointments for Beaverbrook, Simon and Kingsley Wood, and, on Attlee's advice, to see crucial domestic appointments go to Socialists, Bevin (Labour) and Morrison (Supply). Naturally, as time passed, there were considerable changes in personnel, but Churchill never allowed a situation to develop in which any one individual was in a position to replace him. Only in 1942, as measured by Gallup, was public satisfaction with the government less than 50 per cent, and for most of the time more than 70 per cent were apparently satisfied. Significantly, however, Churchill's personal rating was always higher than that of the government, except at the very end of the war. This discrepancy further confirmed that if Churchill were ever to be replaced it would only be likely to be by someone with comparable charisma. The name of Stafford Cripps was sometimes mentioned, a man as distinctively ascetic as Churchill was sybaritic, but it was never a serious possibility. Churchill stayed in power because, looked at negatively, there was no one better, taken in the round, to replace him. Looked at positively, his record suggested that he should remain.

ii. Style and Substance

On 3 September 1939 Winston toasted 'Victory'. In his first speech as Prime Minister on 13 May 1940 he could offer nothing but 'blood, toil, tears and sweat' in pursuit of this objective. It was to be 'victory, victory at all costs, victory in spite of all terror, victory however long and hard the road may be'. He well knew that he was only Prime Minister because of the war. His Great War experience had shown him that the fortunes of a politician at war were even more fickle than usual. The conventions of parliament and the patterns of party were, however, given. They could be tinkered with here and there, but they set the formal parameters of power. The exigencies of war were imperative. Change was necessary and inescapable but it was made manageable and palatable if it occurred within a framework of recognisable continuity.

The need for 'Mobilisation for total war' was well understood. It required a capacity to communicate beyond the confines of cabinet room or debating chamber into hearts and homes which would have preferred a quieter life. It required style. Even those in the political world who had their reservations about Churchill in May 1940, and they were not few in number, acknowledged that he had style. The power of a state at war depended ultimately upon its cohesion and sense of purpose. Churchill saw that very vividly for himself within days of taking office as France fell. He hurried across the Channel seeking to stiffen the will to fight but instead witnessed the crumbling of morale. The extent to which the fall of France was a military failure and the extent to which it was a spiritual disintegration will endlessly be argued over. The lesson for Winston was plain. The power of politicians and generals evaporated if there was no will to fight. In the 1930s he had largely failed to achieve his stated purpose of restoring the will to empire which seemed to be ebbing away from the British elite and people alike. Now, however, with the danger so imminent and so close at hand it would surely be possible to stiffen the sinews and summon up the blood?

Churchill's own subsequent account of *Their Finest Hour* placed an emphasis on a national unity which did not need to be created, merely reinforced in circumstances of stress. In this respect the Prime Minister was the fortunate inheritor of what he regarded as the procrastination and pusillanimity of Baldwin and Chamberlain. A war in 1938 would have been acutely divisive at home – whether or not it would have been successful. It would also have revealed a divided Empire/ Commonwealth. By the time Chamberlain did declare war, the feeling that he had gone to the limit of concession and conciliation was general. War was justified. The only opposition came from Communists in the wake of the Nazi-Soviet Pact. There were some pacifists and conscientious objectors, but not on the scale envisaged during the heady days of the Peace Pledge Union.

There was, therefore, consensus in large measure. The language of Churchillian rhetoric could build on an assumption of the desirability of 'victory' that was almost universal. The orator did not need to convince or controvert. His decades of experience as a public speaker were now put to their most effective use. Half a century later the words on the printed page still have a capacity to move, even though they seem to belong to a different age. The man and the moment were matched. Churchill was old enough to deliver in an old tradition but not too old to be able to adapt himself to the needs of the microphone and the broadcast. It had long rankled with him that the BBC had denied him air time to express his views on India. Now he made up for lost time. No doubt the speeches were not all listened to in reverential silence and they did not all provide instant uplift, but there is ample and diverse testimony to the encouragement they provided. The fact that the English language as Churchill used it did not quite correspond to the way in which anybody actually spoke did not seem to matter.[8] To suggest that Churchill's 'greatest single contribution to the war was his oratory' may be an overstatement, but his speeches were indeed exercises in power of a peculiarly personal kind.[9] Nobody else could emulate them.

Words alone, however, could not suffice. It was necessary to convey a sense of unflagging commitment on the part of

the Prime Minister, but a commitment that was at the same
time cheerful and optimistic. He had to be seen to be out and
about, not bunkered into oblivion. To create such an image
did not entail tampering with reality. For the most part
Churchill was resilient and unflagging. The projection of this
spirit, however, was helped by the Prime Minister's innate
predilection for a good picture. In the past his penchant for
dressing up had occasioned much controlled mirth amongst
those around him. Now its full value became apparent. One
day he was a model of sombre sartorial rectitude, the next he
appeared almost raffishly casual. He could appear by turns
civilian, soldier and sailor. He could be seen on board
innumerable ships, in the desert, at street corners. He had a
stack of hats and caps for all occasions. He may not always
have continued to change his shirts three times a day, but he
would like to have done. The cumulative effect was impressive.
Here was not one man fitting one role but many men filling
many roles – all mysteriously called Winston Churchill. And
everybody knew, or thought they knew, that he always
smoked a cigar. He had an unerring ability to guide himself
through smouldering planks and winding hosepipes with his
ubiquitous walking stick. He would surely guide the nation to
victory. He became 'Good old Winnie' without ever becoming
a man of the people. A man who expected his servant to
squeeze his toothpaste on to his toothbrush continued to live
in sublime ignorance of 'ordinary life', but what did that
matter?

The substance was not at variance with the style. There
are numerous testimonies to the galvanising effect which his
presence had in Whitehall. We are given the spectacle of
respectable civil servants running along the corridors. Regular
office hours and weekends ceased to exist. He worked his
official Civil Service aides hard and had alongside him old
cronies such as Major Morton and Professor Lindemann.
Occasional visitors, like the young scientist R.V. Jones, have
written that they came away with 'the feeling of being
recharged by contact with a source of living power'. Such
recollections cannot be discounted, yet common sense suggests that in the complex bureaucracy of wartime Whitehall
there was a limit to the top-up service which the Prime
Minister could provide. Despite the impression sometimes
conveyed in his memoirs and reinforced by the famous red

'Action this Day' labels, the Prime Minister did not have the power directly to ensure the immediate implementation of all his wishes. His staff officers did their best and Churchill used his accumulated knowledge of 'ways and means' built up over a lifetime to good effect. Even so, a little scepticism does not come amiss. There were an awful lot of people in Whitehall and in the various theatres of conflict who did not 'work with Churchill' and who kept things going, more or less efficiently, who did not keep diaries, and who scarcely ever saw the Prime Minister.[10] And for some who did see him, his hours and methods of work proved not so much stimulating as merely exhausting. The collective power of a group was in danger of being undermined by the dynamo at the hub. That said, the abiding impression remains of a work-horse second to none. A man in his late sixties sustained a working week of some ninety hours for five years, and succeeded in brushing off a heart attack and a bout of pneumonia, both of which might have killed a younger and ostensibly fitter man. His capacity to do the job depended, ultimately, on a physical constitution which seemed largely able to endure the demands which, both gratuitously and inevitably, he placed upon it.[11]

iii. 'The Mountain-tops of Control'

Churchill was a Prime Minister who combined personal battlefield experience in Europe, Africa and Asia, two spells as First Lord of the Admiralty, and a lifelong interest in military history. In one sense, at a moment of crisis, it equipped him uniquely to exercise power effectively. In another, this very experience raised explosive constitutional and practical issues of command and control which could nullify that benefit. Should there be any limit to the power of the Prime Minister at such a juncture?

Churchill knew more about the problems of strategic planning and inter-Service cooperation than anyone else in the forefront of British politics. He had watched from the outside the pre-war attempts to coordinate defence and, in the final months of his government, Chamberlain, in asking him to chair the deliberations of the Chiefs of Staff, made him *de facto* Minister of Defence. When he became Prime Minister, Churchill called himself Minister of Defence (no such post existed in the Great War and its powers were not closely defined).There was no Ministry of Defence, but Churchill relied on what he called his 'handling machine' in the person of General Hastings Ismay, his 'Chief Staff Officer', and a small secretariat. What the appointment signified was a determination to centralise and integrate policy and strategy. With luck, it would be possible to avoid a fiasco like the Dardanelles. Ismay kept Churchill briefed on the work of the Chiefs of Staff Committee (which had been formed back in 1924) though the Prime Minister often attended in person. Over the Chiefs of Staff stood the Defence Committee (Operations) on which sat the Deputy Prime Minister (Attlee), the three Service Ministers (with the Chiefs in attendance) and, later, the Foreign Secretary, with other ministers as the occasion required. Ismay described this outcome, which remained basically intact throughout the war, though the full Defence Committee was latterly called less frequently, as a system which allowed the Prime Minister to exercise a personal, direct, ubiquitous and continuous supervision both over the formulation of policy and military operations in general.

This integrated command structure did not prevent Churchill taking advice elsewhere, but he did not appoint any independent principal strategic adviser. Professor Lindemann was on hand in 11 Downing Street to help with anything, particularly with statistics, if needed. The intimate character of this arrangement enabled Churchill, as he liked, to deal directly with the men who had the responsibility. There is, however, no command structure which does not have its drawbacks as well as its advantages.The extent of the Prime Minister's involvement meant that when things were going badly he could not hold himself at a distance and reshuffle the Minister of Defence. By the same token, he could bask in the credit when things were going well. The structure always made him vulnerable to two contradictory criticisms (both expressed in the vote of no confidence debate of July 1942). He could be accused of excessive collegiality, of declining to act because of opposition from the Chiefs of Staff or the Defence Committee, or he could be accused of excessive interference in operational matters which were best left to the Chiefs of Staff to decide. Neither criticism could crystallise into a firm principle. There was always a balance to be struck and where it rested at any given point depended on the issue on hand and on the tenacity or timidity of those who engaged in debate with the Prime Minister. 'I never wielded autocratic powers', Churchill wrote in his memoirs,'and always had to move with and focus political and professional opinion.'[12] Needless to say, on occasion, he was more inclined to move against rather than to move with that opinion, but he did not make abstract and aloof decisions. He dealt with men (and just occasionally with a woman) in person and, where possible, on the spot.

The personalities of Ironside, followed by Dill (Army), Newall, followed by Portal (Air) and Pound (Navy) were not such as to raise fierce opposition to a determined Prime Minister in his first eighteen months in office. Churchill knew that like any newcomer he would have a honeymoon period during which he could be excused failures because his predecessor could be blamed. That period of grace would not last very long, so he had to make his mark on decisions from the beginning. Even so, in 1940, it was difficult to see what the Defence Committee could do except 'hang on'. Nothing he could have done would have prevented the fall of France, not even the despatch of additional RAF fighters. If he had sent them, their loss might have been fatal to success in the ensuing Battle of Britain. The 'miracle' of the British evacuation from Dunkirk could not disguise the fact that Germany seemed to have gained an enormous advantage. How could a British army ever reconquer the continent? There was no immediate, and perhaps no long-term, answer to that question.

Churchill concentrated instead on the defence of the island: the RAF to hold the skies and the Royal Navy to keep open the sea lanes. His famous tribute, 'Never in the field of human conflict was so much owed by so many to so few', was the culmination of a determined effort on his part to draw public attention to the crucial role of air power. It led him also to the belief that Bomber Command, the sole offensive weapon at British disposal, would prove devastating. The impress of the Prime Minister, light or deep, on all decisions during the 'year of survival' makes it doubly difficult to stand back and ask the counterfactual question: what difference did he make? Arguably the options were so limited that even a man of power of Churchill's stamp could only make choices within a narrow band. He talked on the day the evacuation of Dunkirk ended about the need to avoid the completely defensive habit of mind which he believed had ruined the French. Yet what could he do? Some decisions, however, have an ineradicable (and ruthless) personal stamp about them, notably the decision in July 1940 to sink French warships on the grounds of the threat they posed to British survival if they fell into Axis hands. That was Churchill at war.[13]

Churchill's determination can also be seen in another controversial act, his dismissal of Wavell from command in the Middle East and North Africa in June 1941. 'I wanted to show my power', Desmond Morton records Churchill as saying. The Prime Minister's system required not only intimate contact with the Chiefs of Staff but also a personal relationship with Commanders-in-Chief in the field. He expected them to engage with him. After their first meeting in August 1940 Churchill felt that Wavell lacked the mental vigour and resolve to overcome obstacles which were indispensable to successful war. Moments of satisfaction with Wavell, as after his defeat of the Italians at Sidi Barrani, gave way to increasing impatience with his caution amidst the setbacks of the spring and early summer of 1941. For his part, Wavell felt that while the Prime Minister might be at home in the world of grand strategy, he had little understanding of the operational problems of mechanical warfare in the desert.

Auchinleck, Wavell's replacement, was to meet with the same fate. Field commanders in 1940–41 were subjected to a never-ending stream of memoranda, sometimes hourly. It was a degree of supervision which Marlborough, held up on occasion to the generals as an example, would never have endured. Its positive side was that commanders could also derive encouragement from the feeling that they were engaged in a common enterprise. The Great War rift between 'brasshats' and 'frocks' did not return. With a general like Alexander, also an aristocrat who liked painting, Churchill's communications were in general excellent. That was even the case, despite flash-points, with another more brittle Ulsterman, Bernard Montgomery. Churchill constantly harped on the need to take risks and show flair; field commanders would have liked to have been able to make their own assessments of risks without having to defend them to a man thousands of miles away in London who seemed to think that he knew more than they did. He often did.

It fell to the Chiefs of Staff to try to hold the ring and, on the whole, they did so successfully throughout the duration of the war. Their professional solidarity could never bring the generals to approve of the Prime Minister's 'interference' with their colleagues in the field. All they could do was to seek to argue each case on its merits. There remained no doubt who was in the driving seat. 'It takes a lot of moral courage', Dill wrote to him, 'not to be afraid of being thought afraid.'[14] Churchill sent him off to Washington and he was replaced by Alan Brooke, 'Brookie', in late 1941. This relationship between men of contrasting temperament was pivotal for the rest of the war; scarcely six hours passed without their meeting. There were, of course, thousands of issues that clamoured for attention.[15] There was constant give and take in a fashion which prevents a simplistic assessment of power. Historians can point to instances when Churchill allowed himself to be overruled or at least dissuaded from particular actions – when he should not have done. They can also point to instances when he insisted on going ahead – when he should not have done. On the whole, it was probably beneficial that one who inhabited the 'mountain-tops of control' should so frequently descend into the desert of detail.

iv. The Equipment of Power

It would have been possible: to ensure national commitment; to become an effective communicator; to fashion a reliable command structure; to choose dynamic field commanders – and yet to have lost the battle. It was important to have in place the most effective structures and mechanisms, and the decisions a Prime Minister made in these areas could cumulatively make a major difference to the conduct of the war. Yet one of Churchill's great virtues as a war leader was his awareness of war's unpredictability. What was a source of strength at one moment became vulnerable or obsolete in the next. There is no more difficult task before politician and historian alike than to sift and weigh all those facets of national life and organisation which, when fused, constitute a nation's power to wage effective war. Churchill did not subject them to formal analysis, but his long experience of government, during which he had so conspicuously shown an unwillingness to 'departmentalise' his thinking, revealed the inter-relatedness of absolutely everything.

It also revealed the stark fact, looking at the war Churchill was facing in his first year in office, that Britain did not have sufficient military or economic power to win. Hitler was master of Central and Western Europe. The consolatory evacuation from Dunkirk could not really disguise the rout of the Franco-British armies. The United Kingdom had a population of only 48 million. It was impossible to believe that even an expanded British army could invade the European mainland and inflict a comprehensive defeat on German forces. The efforts of the Royal Navy and of Fighter Command in the summer and autumn of 1940 enabled Britain to survive, but the prospect of 'large scale offensive amphibious operations' was whistling in the dark. The level of shipping losses suggested a different preoccupation. The productive base of the British economy was unequal to the task on hand. Orders for aircraft, other equipment and munitions had already been placed in the United States, but they would have to be paid for. The liquidation of saleable British assets and a running down of the gold reserves would be necessary, but such a process could not go on indefinitely. Estimates naturally varied about the length of time which would elapse before a condition of national bankruptcy was reached – perhaps a year or eighteen months at best. These estimates anteceded the impact of the fall of France.

It was a situation which presented Churchill with the most problematic exercise of power in his whole career. American assistance, in some form, was vital, but could it be achieved on a basis which, in the longer term, ensured the independence and integrity of the British Empire? In the short term, would it be possible to alert Washington to Britain's grave position without painting the picture so darkly that elements in the United States would say that it would be useless to give Britain help? New Treasury forecasts brought forward the date of the exhaustion of Britain's gold and dollar reserves.

Churchill had assiduously cultivated a correspondence with Roosevelt since his return to the Admiralty. Over the months and years that followed it was to prove an exchange of letters of rare fascination and importance.[16] The authors mixed their political comment with some personal observations and a degree of intimacy was established – though Winston was irritated that the President supposed his ancestor was 'Marl-boro'. Yet both men were manoeuvring for position throughout. Churchill was a supplicant, but was a proud supplicant. Roosevelt was sympathetic but had no intention of simply underwriting the British position in the world. Domestically, the British would have to be seen to be paying a price for whatever help they might receive. The fate of the Royal Navy in the event of a German invasion was a matter of concern. Hence, after months of negotiation in the summer of 1940, an agreement was reached to furnish the British with fifty elderly American destroyers. The Americans, in return, could lease a string of Atlantic and Caribbean bases.

After Roosevelt was re-elected in November 1940, much effort on the British side went into a lengthy letter of 7 December which set out the gravity of the position. It emphasised the losses at sea and the impending exhaustion of dollar credits. Surely the United States would not wish to see Britain 'stripped to the bone' by the attainment of victory? It was claimed that the letter was not an appeal for aid but rather a statement of the minimum action necessary to the achievement 'of our common purpose'. An earlier draft had attempted to make the cooperation more explicit. The only hope of a 'reasonably liberal world' after the war was for the United States and Great Britain to possess 'unquestionable air and sea supremacy'. Power in the hands of these two great liberal nations offered the only stable prospect of peace. In such an enterprise neither country should be 'placed in the position of being the suppliant client of the other'.[17] Such a plea for equal partnership sounded well. The reality, as the British ambassador expressed it, was that Britain was 'broke'. Roosevelt was not to be pushed but he sent Harry Hopkins to London as a personal representative. Hopkins confirmed that assistance would not be wasted – a rather different impression had been coming from the about to be replaced US Ambassador, Joseph Kennedy. The way was open for 'Lend-Lease' in the spring of 1941. The act allowed the US President, with cash from Congress, to procure through US service departments or buying agencies, supplies which might be 'lent' or 'leased' to any country whose defence the President deemed vital to the defence of the United States. No cash payment was required from the recipient government for such goods, though, later, the British government was to be required to reduce trade barriers at the end of the war. The two 'great English-speaking democracies' were indeed getting more 'mixed up' with each other. Churchill described this legislation in public as 'the most unsordid act' in history. In private, on 20 March, he wrote to his Chancellor of the Exchequer that it appeared as if the terms meant that Britain was 'not only to be skinned, but flayed to the bone'.[18] He added that he would like to get the Americans 'hooked a little firmer, but they are pretty well on now. The power of the debtor is in the ascendant, especially when he is doing all the fighting.' It was an odd way to interpret a step which was 'the end of Britain's career as a self-sufficient great power'.

The debtor power, in addition, was only to do all the fighting for a few more months. On 22 June, German forces invaded the Soviet Union. Churchill's reaction was firm. He was no doubt relieved at this 'diversion' after a series of setbacks over the previous six months, most recently in Crete. Despite his long hostility to Communism, which he did not retract, he confirmed that the cause of any Russian fighting for his hearth and his home, as he put it, was the cause of free men and free peoples in every part of the globe. Russia should be given 'all the aid in Britain's power'. In the months that followed the provision of such aid was to prove both difficult and dangerous, but in all the circumstances more than just words of support was required. It was important that Stalin should not conclude that Britain was powerless, but the realities of British power placed severe limitations on assistance. Both countries committed themselves against a separate peace. Churchill did not underestimate the importance of the survival of the Soviet Union. A complete German success in the East would enable the knock-out blow against Britain to be delivered. No British troops, however, were to be sent to fight alongside the Red Army but the prospect of a bombing offensive was held out, just at the point when doubts about the impact of bombing were in fact being raised. Stalin sent Churchill a birthday telegram but, apart from this gesture, no epistolary intimacy developed between the two men to compare with that which existed between Churchill and Roosevelt.

In August 1941 Churchill and Roosevelt went one stage further. They met on board ship off the coast of Newfoundland at a spot where, significantly, an American base was being built. In the context of wide-ranging discussions – which did not include the possibility of the United States entering the war- the two leaders drew up a portentous 'Atlantic Charter' (really a press release) which set out the principles which should guide a post-war settlement in a war in which the United States was neutral. The most troublesome aspect, from Churchill's standpoint, was the pledge to 'respect the right of all peoples to choose the form of government under which they will live'. He could not believe that this admirable principle applied to Asia, Africa or the Middle East. The mixture of anxiety and elation which Churchill experienced at this meeting, which reflected the ambiguities of power existing at the time, was paralleled and heightened by the Japanese strike against Pearl Harbor on 7 December. Three days later Churchill, having committed Britain to fight Japan, departed for Washington to offer advice. A direct Japanese attack on the United States was more than he had hoped for: 'So we had won after all!'

Who was the 'we'? Between May 1940 and June 1941 the power Churchill wielded was the fractured power of the British Empire. For the previous six months, however, it had been the Soviet Union which had absorbed German military might – and, with a bit of luck, had succeeded in withstanding it. There would be a long struggle ahead in Eastern Europe but if the Red Army drove German forces back, Stalin would not be reluctant to claim victory. Did Churchill include him in his 'we'? He was explicit that it was a common foe which brought the two countries together, despite their profound differences. What happened when the foe was vanquished? Churchill was much more ready to believe that Britain and the United States shared the same values, but the underlying tensions have already been indicated. The events of December 1941 brought Britain and the United States together openly, but left unresolved the issues of power inherent in their relationship. Actual conflict in Asia, too, threatened to expose the hollowness of British power in the Indian sub-continent and Malaya and, with it, the fraudulent nature of the support Britain could offer Australia and New Zealand.

Dating back to his days as post-war Colonial Secretary, when he acquiesced, under United States and Dominion pressure, in the non-renewal of the Anglo-Japanese treaty of alliance, Churchill had been somewhat relaxed about the

Japanese position in East Asia. He seems to have supposed that the Japanese would not in fact attack, that if they did they would not be a match for a Western opponent, and finally that the United States would deter them. All of these assumptions had been or were about to be proved false. Prior to Pearl Harbor, the alarming possibility had been of a Japanese attack on British possessions to which the Americans would not feel obliged to respond. Churchill tried to interest Roosevelt in the use of the Singapore base by the US Navy, but he met with no success. It was tantamount to an admission, to which Wellington and Canberra were not privy, that, earlier promises to the contrary notwithstanding, if hostilities did break out, commitments elsewhere would mean that in fact Britain would not be able to despatch major additional naval forces to South-East Asia. Churchill did not come to this conclusion joyfully, but he felt sure that Australia and New Zealand would understand the priority of Europe and the Mediterranean, as they always had done.

In fact, however, Churchill had decided to send the *Prince of Wales* and *Repulse* to Singapore. On 10 December 1941, two days before he departed for Washington, Churchill received the shocking news that they had been sunk. Once again, air power had been underestimated. More shocking news followed, culminating in the fall of Singapore in February 1942 – 'the greatest military disaster in British history'. It came on top of German gains in North Africa and the escape of the German battle cruisers *Scharnhorst* and *Gneisenau* from Brest. Early in March, Rangoon fell. The gains made in the 'Crusader' campaign in North Africa were nullified and in June Tobruk, with its defenders and stores, fell to the German commander, Rommel. Further, these setbacks in different parts of the world exposed even more conspicuously the frailty and imminent disintegration of the British Empire. The defenders of Tobruk – Australians, South Africans, Indians and British – were the 'we' who were to win the war, but this sense of collective Britishness was attenuating. The Australian government was furious at the turn of events in South-East Asia and was henceforth determined to put 'Australia First' – in conjunction with the United States. The South Africans, all along, had their own priorities. India was in confusion. Cripps had been sent out in March to try to secure the cooperation of Indian political leaders in return for post-war independence, but the mission failed. Disturbances in August were contained with difficulty and Gandhi, Nehru and other leaders were interned. It is not surprising, in the light of these signs of loss of British power, that Churchill faced parliamentary criticism.

Montgomery's victory at El Alamein at the beginning of November 1942 stopped the slide in Churchill's political standing. 'I have not become the King's First Minister', he declared a week later, 'in order to preside over the liquidation of the British Empire.'[19] It was a bold declaration but one that was to prove impossible to honour. In that same month, the 'Torch' landings took place in North-West Africa in an operation significantly commanded by the American, Eisenhower. It was true that Churchill had advocated this step but the Americans were to supply the men, as they were in increasing millions worldwide as the war progressed. In the same month, the Red Army began a winter offensive that was to culminate in the victory of Stalingrad in the spring of 1943. The writing was on the wall for Hitler but so, in a different sense, was it for Churchill.

From this point on, as the power of the United States and the Soviet Union waxed, so that of the British Empire waned. Churchill sensed a different climate but did not quite know how to react to it. His sense of power was always strongly personal. It was no accident that he had been and was still to be the biggest traveller of any major political figure during the war. The power of personality could compensate for the relative decline in imperial strength. 'It was my duty to go', Churchill telegrammed to Attlee at the conclusion of his visit to Stalin in August 1942. 'Now they know the worst . . .' He was sure that 'the disappointing news I brought [concerning a Second Front] could not have been imparted except by me personally without leading to really serious drifting apart'.[20] The conference with Roosevelt at Casablanca in January 1943, most well-known for its announcement that the Allies required Germany's 'unconditional surrender', was another example of 'the personal touch'. Churchill painted a picture in Marrakesh which he presented to the President as a gesture of friendship. There were further conferences at Washington and in Quebec in May and August 1943 before the year climaxed with the first 'Big Three' conference at Teheran at the end of the year.

Such 'summit diplomacy' taxed Churchill's physical strength and had both its advantages and disadvantages. Perhaps it was the prospect of victory rather than the avoidance of defeat which led him, particularly at Quebec, to put forward plans dealing with areas as diverse as the Dutch East Indies and Norway. It seemed to Americans that he was still reluctant to give 'Overlord', the invasion of France, the complete priority which they thought it demanded. It was an indication of the realities of power, however, that Churchill agreed to the appointment of an American as supreme commander of the Allied armies in the field in Normandy. He had previously promised Brooke the job and, to Brooke's chagrin, never explained what had happened – perhaps because he could not himself quite come to terms with the significance of this appointment.

The atmosphere at Teheran led Churchill to telegraph to Attlee that 'relations between Britain, United States and USSR have never been so cordial and intimate. All war plans are agreed and concerted.' This confident statement glossed over the differences concerning Poland, Italy, and 'Overlord', to name only three areas. 'The real problem now is Russia', Churchill had told Harold Macmillan on the eve of the conference. 'I *can't* get the Americans to see it.' He also could not get the Americans to feel happy about the maintenance of British power in the Middle East and in South-East Asia. Indeed, many Americans saw Britain as still committed to trade barriers, colonialism and 'spheres of influence' which presented as great an obstacle to future peace and security as the Soviet Union. After Teheran, Roosevelt had further talks with Churchill in Cairo and to some extent the old intimacy appeared to be restored. However, it is not altogether fanciful to see in the bad pneumonia to which Churchill then suc-cumbed, and which almost killed him, an indication of his own sense of failure and relative political debility.

From 1944 onwards, therefore, he acted as second fiddle in an American-directed effort. He never quite adjusted himself to this position and his mood – and opinions – could lurch quite wildly. The success of the Normandy landings could be seen, fundamentally, as a marvellous example of British-American cooperation, despite the inevitable friction here and there. In such a context, all the old rhetoric about the two 'English-speaking democracies' could be again rehearsed. Yet

American pressure against the kind of Empire Churchill believed in remained constant. It was also the case that serious differences with Washington existed on future Allied strategy in the Mediterranean. On the other hand, Britain and the United States might yet order the post-war world. But then again perhaps the Americans might not stay in Europe after the defeat of Germany? And, whether they did or did not, it began to look as though their ubiquitous stress upon 'Freedom' would be distressing. In November 1944, for example, Churchill found himself under pressure to agree to American plans for civil airlines to compete for traffic in a free market. He was told that Congress would not be in a generous mood concerning 'lend-lease' if 'the people feel that the United Kingdom has not agreed to a generally beneficial air agreement'. Churchill sent a lengthy rejoinder which concluded by stating that he had

> never advocated competitive "Bigness" in any sphere between our two countries in their present state of development. You will have the greatest navy in the world. You will have, I hope, the greatest air force. You will have the greatest trade. You have all the gold.[21]

However, these things did not frighten him because he was sure that the American people would not entertain vainglorious ambitions and that justice and fair-play would guide them. Such certainty was not universal in wartime London.

This bundle of conflicting hopes and interpretations was matched by similar ambiguities about the Soviet Union. Stalin's brutal indifference, or so it seemed, to the fate of the Warsaw Rising appalled Churchill, but on the other hand he felt that Stalin was a man with whom he could and should do business.[22] He told his publisher that he would not deliver a book he had contracted to write in 1939 on *Europe since the Russian Revolution*: 'Am I to bring up the horrors of the Russian Revolution? My whole outlook is changed. The synopsis which was a living thing then is now dead. Twenty Years' Alliance with Russia.'[23] After another visit to Quebec he set off for Moscow. There, on half a sheet of paper, he reached a 'percentages' agreement with Stalin which supposedly settled their respective predominances in Roumania, Greece, Yugoslavia, Hungary and Bulgaria. Churchill described his list as a 'naughty document' which would have shocked the Americans.[24] However, he was sure that Marshal Stalin was a realist. He himself was not sentimental. The twinkle in each other's eyes suggested that they understood each other. They moved on to discuss Poland, on which matter, to the dismay of the London Poles, Churchill came to understand that he could do little, at least without full American support – in one of his more exasperated remarks he told angry Poles that Great Britain was no bigger than Poland. The subsequent telegram to President Roosevelt, after the conversation concerning the Balkans, made no reference to the sort of agreement he and Stalin had in mind. Although the Americans did not like Churchill's subsequent interventions in the internal affairs of Greece, he found that Stalin in this respect more or less honoured the realism of their October bargain. Churchill came back to tell his colleagues in the Cabinet on 27 November 1944 that Russia 'was ready and anxious to work in with us. No immediate threat of war lay ahead of us once the present war was over.'[25]

The Yalta conference of February 1945 at first seemed to give grounds for optimism. It was to be the last and most expansive meeting of the men of power. Stalin toasted Churchill as 'the man who is born once in a hundred years' and 'the bravest statesman in the world'. There was liberal consumption of what Sir Alexander Cadogan, the Permanent Under-Secretary at the Foreign Office, believed to be Caucasian champagne.[26] In the full flow of imminent victory there seemed astonishingly widespread agreement – on the future of the new World Organisation, on arrangements for the occupation of Germany, in which France was to have a zone alongside 'the Big Three', on the return of prisoners of war, and other matters. Only on the question of the composition of the Polish government was there major continuing disagreement. Churchill seemed pleased with the outcome. Nevertheless, in the final weeks of the war, despite the affable manner of 'Uncle Joe', Churchill grew more anxious about the Soviet Union. The final disposition of forces would not be an insignificant factor in the bargains which would still need to be struck. He proved unable to carry much weight – the very success of the integrated allied command precluded any special British adventures on any serious scale. The German surrender was accepted on 8 May 1945. The great power struggle in Europe was over.[27]

The mixture of idealism and ruthlessness, of romanticism and realism which had informed Churchill's understanding of political power for decades is confirmed in these exchanges. Part of him rather liked behaving like an imperial potentate and disposing of the future of whole countries on the back of an envelope. Part of him had an enthusiasm for traditional monarchy. Part of him was quite prepared to back a Communist, as in the case of Tito of Yugoslavia, if there appeared to be military advantages in doing so. Part of him looked forward to a future World Organisation and a world without war, even, in one conversation, to a civilisation which would conform to the prescriptions of the Sermon on the Mount. Part of him delighted in driving round Athens at Christmastime in an armoured car with a pistol in his hand. Part of him rhapsodised about the English-speaking peoples and supposed that there was more in the internal logic of the British-American relationship than was inherently likely. Part of him hated what the Americans would do to the British Empire. In this respect, as the European war ended, he was particularly anxious for a share in the final action against Japan as an indication that Britain would re-establish a South-East Asian empire even if, in the end, India had to be given up. Part of him feared that power had gone from the island race for good. In November 1944 he could not see how 'we could maintain an Expeditionary Army of 50 or 60 divisions, which is the least required to play in the Continental war game'.[28]

Even as he wrote these words, part of him glimpsed a new kind of power, an atomic bomb, which could play havoc with all conventional military assumptions. Its development, however, was another indication of the way the wind was blowing. Early work on the project for an atomic bomb had begun in Britain but then transferred to the United States where greater resources for its development were available. In the latter stages of the war Churchill fought against American attempts to restrict British access to atomic information to which he was entitled. In 1945, however, Britain was to have no control over the atomic bombs that were dropped on Hiroshima and Nagasaki.[29] The whole of him hated Communism but the whole of him could not resist admiration for the Russian people who had done so much to make victory possible. It was a source of great pleasure that Clementine Churchill broadcast to the Russian people from Moscow on her husband's behalf, expressing his hope that the two countries might 'in loyal comradeship and sympathy walk in the sunshine of victorious peace'.

It remained to be seen whether he would be the man to shape the destiny of the island race in the difficult times that would inevitably follow the euphoria of victory.

. . .

NOTES AND REFERENCES

1. Martin Gilbert, *Winston S. Churchill*, Volume V, p. 1111.
2. S.W. Roskill, *Churchill and the Admirals*, London, 1977, pp. 88–9.
3. K.G. Robbins, *Appeasement*, Oxford, 1988.
4. M. Gilbert, *Winston S. Churchill*, London, 1991, p. 637.
5. The latest discussion of this contentious sequence of events is Andrew Roberts, *'The Holy Fox': A Biography of Lord Halifax*, London, 1991, pp. 197–207.
6. J.M. Lee, *The Churchill Coalition 1940–1945*, London, 1980.
7. David Day, 'Churchill and his War Rivals', *History Today*, April 1991, pp. 15–21. Dr Day's *Menzies and Churchill at War*, London, 1986, provides material on the extent to which the Australian politician presented a 'threat'.
8. Piers Brendon, *Winston Churchill*, London, 1984, p. 144. See also David Cannadine's perceptive introduction to his edition of *Churchill's Speeches*, Harmondsworth, 1990.
9. See Ian McLaine, *Ministry of Morale: Home Front Morale and the Ministry of Information in World War II*, London, 1979, p. 99.
10. See Sir John Wheeler-Bennett, ed., *Action This Day: Working with Churchill*, London, 1968; Sir John Colville, *The Churchillians*, London, 1981, and *The Fringes of Power: Downing Street Diaries 1939–1955*, London, 1985; Raymond A. Callahan, *Churchill: Retreat from Empire*, Tunbridge Wells, 1984, makes the point that Churchill could not control every facet of government, despite his general supervision of affairs.
11. Charles Wilson, Lord Moran, *Winston Churchill: The Struggle for Survival 1940–1965*, London, 1966. This useful work by Churchill's doctor is controversial because, as he

himself admits, he did not keep a diary 'in the ordinary sense of the word'.

12. Cited and discussed by Liddell Hart in A.J.P. Taylor, ed., *Churchill: Four Faces and the Man*, London, 1969, p. 197.

13. Patrick Cosgrave, Churchill at War, Vol. 1, *Alone 1939–1940*, London, 1974; David Jablonsky, *Churchill, The Great Game and Total War*, London, 1991, illustrates his thesis that Churchill carried the Victorian tension between romanticism and pragmatism in his extension of the 'Great Game' into World War II, p. 143.

14. Alex Danchev, ' "Dilly-Dally", or Having the Last Word: Field Marshal Sir John Dill and Prime Minister Winston Churchill', *Journal of Contemporary History*, Vol. 22, No.1, January 1987.

15. Sir Arthur Bryant's editions of Alanbrooke's diaries, *The Turn of the Tide*, London, 1957, and *Triumph in the West*, London, 1959, constituted the first substantial non-Churchillian perspective on the war. They were not to Churchill's liking.

16. Warren F. Kimball, *Churchill and Roosevelt: The Complete Correspondence*, 3 vols., Princeton, 1984.

17. Kimball, *Churchill and Roosevelt*, Volume ii, pp. 87–111.

18. Martin Gilbert, *'Finest Hour': Winston S. Churchill*, Volume VI, *1939–1941*, London, 1983. p. 1040.

19. Gilbert, *'Road to Victory': Winston S. Churchill*, Volume VII, *1941–1945*, London, 1986, p. 254.

20. *Ibid.* p.206

21. Kimball, *Churchill and Roosevelt*, Volume iii, p. 421.

22. According to Dalton's diary, Churchill was making firm statements at this time that Russian friendship could be maintained as long as Stalin lasted. 'Poor Neville Chamberlain believed he could trust Hitler. He was wrong. But I don't think I'm wrong about Stalin.' B. Pimlott, ed., *The Second World War Diary of Hugh Dalton 1940–45*, London, 1986, p. 836.

23. Gilbert, *op.cit.*, pp. 949–50

24. Graham Ross, ed., *The Foreign Office and the Kremlin: British Documents on Anglo-Soviet Relations 1941–45*, Cambridge, 1984, p. 177.

25. Gilbert, *op.cit.*, p. 1071.

26. D. Dilks ed., *The Diaries of Sir Alexander Cadogan 1938–1945*, London, 1971, p. 707.

27. David Reynolds, 'Churchill and the British "Decision" to fight on in 1940: right policy, wrong reasons', in R. Langhorne, ed., *Diplomacy & Intelligence during the Second World War: Essays in Honour of F.H. Hinsley*, Cambridge, 1985, pp. 147–67, leads into H.B. Ryan, *The Vision of Anglo-America. The US-UK Alliance and the Emerging Cold War, 1943–1946*, Cambridge, 1987
28. Gilbert, *op.cit.*, p. 1070.
29. Peter Malone, *The British Nuclear Deterrent*, London, 1984, pp. 56–8. Margaret Gowing, 'Britain, America and the Bomb', in M. Dockrill and J.W. Young, eds., *British Foreign Policy 1945–56*, London, 1989, pp.31–46.

Chapter 6

LOSS OF POWER
1945–1955

. . .

DEFIANCE IN DEFEAT

The first general election for ten years was held on 5 July
1945. Earlier, Churchill had been in correspondence with the
Labour leadership about the date and manner in which the
Coalition government should be brought to an end. As a
result, he had resigned on 23 May and then accepted the
King's invitation to form a largely Conservative administration pending the outcome of the election. The preservation
of power might prove a more difficult task than some
supposed.

As has been noted, Churchill had not come to power after
a general election. He only became party leader after he
became Prime Minister. He had led a Coalition government.
Now, however, he wanted the electorate to make him Prime
Minister at the head of the Conservative Party in preference
to leaders of the Labour Party who had been his colleagues in
government for five years. In euphoric moments during the
course of the war Churchill had commented privately on the
sense of solidarity displayed by the nation at large and by
politicians in particular.[1] On such occasions he had seen
himself as a truly national leader and could not contemplate
reversion to the sterile banalities of party conflict. Dalton
recorded in his diary that at an At Home at No.10 on 28 May
1945 Churchill addressed a gathering of colleagues and ex-
colleagues with tears running down his cheeks. They had all
come together and had stayed together as a united band of

friends 'in a very trying time'. Perhaps he would withdraw gracefully from politics with his reputation as 'the man who had won the war' beyond dispute?

By the spring of 1945, however, his enjoyment of power was still conspicuous, the war against Japan had still to be won, and there was another conference of the 'Big Three' scheduled for mid-July. It could not be said that his age or his health seriously incommoded him. Churchill contrasted his experience of international affairs not unfavourably with that of the incoming President Truman. He seems to have thought that he could do business with Stalin as effectively as anyone.[2] In short, he did not seriously consider retirement. It was also the case that no political figure in his entourage or in the Conservative Party had either the courage or the inclination to ask him formally to stand down. Insofar as it could be measured, his international reputation and national standing both remained high. He would surely fight and win the ensuing campaign.

The temptation to fight the election on a personal basis was very strong. The success of Lloyd George in 1918 appeared to offer an encouraging precedent. Churchill had a flamboyance which contrasted with Attlee's more prosaic personality. It was *Mr Churchill's Declaration of Policy* . . . which was offered to the electors. He travelled about the country in a special train and almost without exception was greeted by cheering crowds. The emphasis on Churchill's own personal stature seemed entirely justified. He made four of the ten broadcasts allocated to the Conservatives – Attlee made only one of the ten Labour broadcasts. The broadcasts, in fact, were probably ill-judged and he would have been better advised not to have made so many. Leo Amery was not alone in thinking it a mistake for Winston to have jumped straight off his pedestal as a world statesman 'to deliver a fantastical exaggerated onslaught on Socialism'.[3] Except on the morning of the declaration, however, – for special reasons three weeks after the election – Churchill seems to have had little premonition of defeat.[4] In the event, it was not only a defeat, it was a massive humiliation. Labour had a majority of more than 200 over the Conservatives, a majority which was in no way threatened even if the Ulster Unionists, National Liberals (in effect Conservatives) and Liberals were all to support the Conservatives on particular issues. The scale of the parliamentary majority was misleading insofar as Labour did not quite gain a majority of the votes cast, but the trend of opinion was indisputable. Even before the counting was completed, Churchill submitted his resignation to the King on 26 July and advised him to send for Attlee.

The Labour victory has been much speculated upon ever since – it came as a surprise to some Labour leaders as much as it did to Churchill – and explanations still vary in emphasis.[5] It has been noted that a 'swing of the pendulum' after so many years was not surprising. The Labour Party was perhaps at last resuming the advance which had been shattered by the debacle of 1931. The notion that the forces' vote was of great significance is now widely discounted but Conservatives, searching for an explanation, seized upon the left-wing influence which they detected at work in the Army Bureau of Current Affairs. There may have been, too, a feeling that Lloyd George had not in fact 'won the Peace' particularly convincingly, either domestically or internationally. That suggested an advantage in having a fresh mind brought to bear upon the problems of peacemaking.

Did Churchill contribute personally to the scale of the defeat or without him might it have been even greater? Both at the time and subsequently there have been divergent opinions. *The Manchester Guardian* was not alone in criticising Churchill for turning the election into a 'personal plebiscite'. Even supposing that was what he did, it is still not easy to judge its effect. It may have been the case that a section of the electorate feared that a victorious Churchill would exert too much power. Perhaps unconsciously, he would carry over into peace a way of exercising power which a nation at war should only tolerate exceptionally. He needed to be cut down to size and the only way to do that was to vote against him. In other words, it was his very success which counted against him, however perversely. Some Conservatives may have had this consideration in mind, having not overcome their pre-war suspicion of Churchill's record. On the other hand, it is arguable that Churchill in 1945 was more popular than the Conservative Party and that he therefore enticed many voters to vote for him personally who would not have voted Conservative on any other ground. Against that, it has been widely suggested that Churchill misjudged the mood of the country on domestic issues. His pronouncement that 'no Socialist

system can be established without a political police', that is
to say by a 'Gestapo' (albeit humanely directed at first), was
denounced by Labour as a piece of scaremongering. His
insight in this matter was held to be injudicious at best and a
reminder of a congenital disposition to exaggerate.

Such an observation also heightened the suspicions of those
who thought him 'reactionary' and out of sympathy with the
measures of social reform which had been discussed and
debated since the publication of the Beveridge Report in
December 1942. In the spring of 1943, nearly 100 Labour
MPs had supported an amendment critical of the government's reaction to the proposals in the Report. Opinion polls
at this time gave Labour a big lead over the Conservatives –
a result which probably reflected growing public interest in
the shape of post-war Britain, as it began to be assumed that
the war would be won.[6] Talk about 'full employment', 'a
welfare state' and a house-building programme for the rest of
the war placed the Prime Minister at an increasing disadvantage and began to make apparent the flaws in the coalition
government (from his point of view). Churchill's concern that
Conservatives should on the whole occupy ministries with
responsibility for the direction of the war had its inevitable
corollary. Labour ministers with domestic portfolios became
more familiar to the general public and could be more readily
identified with proposals for 'social improvement'. Although
the contrast should not be overdrawn, it could appear that
the Conservatives were more concerned with 'winning the
war' and Labour with 'winning the peace'.

It was easy to see in the Prime Minister's procrastination
evidence of hostility towards 'Beveridgeism', a suspicion
which was not altogether without foundation. However, his
procrastination was fundamentally the result of a conviction
that the war was far from won and that undue attention to
social proposals, and certainly firm commitment in this area,
was premature. His anxiety went deeper. He warned ministers against the dangers of raising 'false hopes' – instancing in
this respect the mistake 'last time' of talking about 'Homes
for Heroes'.

What concerned him, as the war drew to a close, was its
overall economic impact on the country. At the height of
Britain's determination to fight on, the payment of bills and
the future viability of the British economy had been pushed

on one side. They could not be left there indefinitely. During the greater part of the war Churchill had exercised power with a calculated lack of anxiety, in public, about the economic base which was vital to that power. By 1945 it would be folly to suppose that the immediate and enduring priority could be welfare expenditure. In fact, during the campaign, his comments on family allowances, housing and national insurance in no sense indicated a principled hostility to 'social reform', but in this area Churchill could not make himself sound more ambitious and enthusiastic than Labour. At the end of a long war, an electorate wanted a vision of social transformation rather than an incomprehensible exposition of Britain's economic and industrial prospects. And Churchill himself had to believe that the broad sunlit uplands were not beyond the bounds of possibility.[7]

The loss of power in 1945, whatever weight is given to the factors which occasioned it, came as a staggering surprise to Churchill himself. Of all his many setbacks in his tortuous career there was nothing more humiliating. It might have been more easily endured if he had sheltered behind the banner of his party almost modestly and thus not exposed himself to the verdict of the electors quite so conspicuously. Even in his own constituency, where he was not opposed by either Labour or the Liberals, an Independent who insisted on standing polled well. His wife saw the outcome of the election as the opportunity she had been waiting for to urge retirement. Churchill responded characteristically to the suggestion that his loss of power was a blessing in disguise. The disguise, he declared, was pretty effective. He would carry on.

Even so, it was not clear what he should do. His lack of affection for humdrum opposition has already been noted. It was unlikely that a man in his early seventies would develop a zeal for constant harrying and criticism. The size of Labour's majority indicated that there would be no general election before 1950. It also suggested, in some minds at least, that Labour would be in office indefinitely. The election had produced an irreversible shift in the direction of Socialism. During the campaign Churchill had not only raised the spectre of a political police but also suggested that a future Labour government would be dictated to by the extra-parliamentary National Executive of the Labour Party. The nature of the parliamentary system, as Churchill understood it, appeared to be under threat. Some of Churchill's younger colleagues felt that he overstated the dangers – but, if he was right, they also felt that he could not be the man to mount an effective opposition either in parliament or the country. It is impossible to say how many Conservative MPs wanted him to step down but Churchill resisted any such suggestions. It is equally impossible, however, to tell whether he realistically supposed that he would ever again become Prime Minister.

In the short term, he had two forms of influence, if not of power, which were not always open to the Leader of the Opposition. His wartime record made him a 'world states-man' for all time. There would never be any limit to the honours offered to him in Europe and America – honorary degrees from universities and the freedoms of cities. He could spend all his time travelling and making speeches. Even though he no longer held office he could command attention to an abnormal degree even for an ex-Prime Minister. He remained a 'name' whose drawing power exceeded that of his successor. Churchill did not deliberately set out to break that convention in British politics which requires the Leader of the Opposition to exercise restraint in criticising the government of the day when speaking in a foreign country, but the power he could wield abroad caused some disquiet and resentment amongst members of the Labour government. At worst this was a petty jealousy, at best it was a tenable anxiety that Churchill was 'hi-jacking' issues which were properly the concern of government.

The second role which Churchill was eager to adopt was that of chronicler of his own achievement in the form of volumes on *The Second World War*. He knew, too, that he had a unique position and could use his writings as a means not only of keeping his name in the public eye as the books appeared but also of stamping, possibly for all time, his own perspective on the interpretation of the Second World War. The sales of his book would be likely to ensure that his framework would be far more influential in establishing the origins, pattern and consequences of that war than any other volume conceivably could. Churchill was again willing to concede that his account could not be the definitive history, but it could certainly supply the materials of such a history. In the absence of rival interpretations from Hitler, Roosevelt or Stalin, the pivotal role of Britain could be asserted.

Once again, as with *The World Crisis* and other subsequent books, Churchill showed masterly powers of organisation and self-discipline. He plunged into the operation in September 1945, assisted by his customary bevy of helpers and advisers – though there was never any doubt that he was in control. He was in an extraordinarily advantageous position because he could reproduce or use documentation years before archives were opened or official histories were written. The shape and sequence of material influenced all subsequent writers in the secondary histories of the war which were to appear in the ensuing decades. The speed with which the enterprise was placed before a wide public on both sides of the Atlantic through serialisation and in book form implanted a picture which was to endure at least until Churchill's death. Inevitably, by that date and subsequently, particular interpretations have been challenged. Other prominent figures have published their own memoirs which cast a rather different light from that cast by Churchill on certain episodes, though few of them could write as well as Winston. Churchill avoided controversy on some issues, for example the latter-day bombing of Dresden, by omitting discussion altogether. In addition, he made no reference to the benefits and complications which arose from the possession in London of German signals intelligence. The knowledge it provided significantly shaped Churchill's decisions and gave him an insight into the intentions of the enemy without parallel in the history of war. The information he had from this source, as we now know, makes more comprehensible the reasons for certain courses of action (including what might seem overbearing conduct) which could not be made explicit in his published history at the time, and indeed remained secret until nearly a decade after his death.

The literary and publishing success of the enterprise was beyond question. The former was recognised by the award of the Nobel Prize for Literature in 1953, though later volumes were not much more than compilations of material strung together with little by way of connecting narrative. The combined first impression on both sides of the Atlantic was of the order of 300,000 per volume. Churchill's personal financial position was at long last secure.

The first volume, *The Gathering Storm*, was published in 1948 and gave Churchill the opportunity for which he had long been waiting to write at length on the origins of the war and its course down to the political crisis of May 1940. He could not avoid detecting a beautiful coherence in his own view and expressed it in luminous prose. It was a passionate book and its message was clear. He was describing how the English-speaking peoples, 'through their unwisdom, carelessness and good nature allowed the wicked to re-arm'. There was a lesson here for the year in which the book appeared. Past history and present politics again fused deliberately in Churchill's mind. The year 1948, in which the Communist coup took place in Prague, was a decade on from Munich.

It was in this respect that Churchill's two most prominent roles in the early post-war years came together. In the early months of 1946, having got his history started and leaving the conduct of the Opposition in the hands of Anthony Eden, he left for the United States – fitting in a visit also to Havana where they made exceedingly good cigars. Amongst other engagements, he accepted an invitation to speak at Westminster College, Fulton, Missouri, in March, where he was to be introduced by President Truman.[8] This 'Iron Curtain' speech was to be the most-remembered of all those he made in the post–1945 period. He painted a picture of a curtain descending from Stettin in the Baltic to Trieste in the Adriatic, behind which were all the capitals of the ancient states of Central and Eastern Europe. Police governments prevailed in that region and, except for Czechoslovakia, there was no true democracy.

Of course, Churchill was not the first to notice the existence of this division and he had himself been referring to its significance, to Truman amongst others, privately for many months. From March 1946, however, it was Churchill's 'iron curtain' which became a household term. His primary purpose, however, was to dwell on the 'special relationship', as he called it, between the British Commonwealth and Empire and the United States. The fraternal association of the English-speaking peoples would make possible the sure prevention of war and the continuous rise of the world organisation (the United Nations). In further speeches in Williamsburg, Virginia and in New York, he stated that he had never asked for an Anglo-American military alliance or treaty. What he pleaded for was a union of hearts based upon conviction and common ideals. Churchill's renewed stress upon the 'special relationship' (another of his phrases that was to stick) was highly significant. The cooling of his relationship with Roosevelt, symbolised in the fact that he did not go to Roosevelt's funeral, had been put behind him in his anxiety about the intentions of the erstwhile 'Uncle Joe'.[9]

The rhetorical activities of Churchill in the United States in the spring of 1946 mark a significant step in the emerging 'Cold War'. He was anxious to halt any tendency towards isolation in the United States and his stress upon the 'special relationship' was in the context of further American restrictions upon British access to information about the atomic bomb. Two years on, *The Gathering Storm*, with its explicit reference to the shortcomings of the English-speaking peoples, and not merely to British shortcomings, rubbed home the same point. At the same time, the Americans were to understand from his narrative that they should never underestimate the British, even when they appeared to be floundering. He had been right about Hitler in 1938; he was now right about Stalin in 1948.

After a few speeches at Westminster on his return from the United States, Churchill again left Britain for the European mainland. He once more made use of occasions when civic and academic honours were showered on him to make headline-catching speeches. The theme he developed in Europe between May and September 1946 was at first sight surprising – the United States of Europe. His speech in Zurich in September 1946 used that specific term and advocated in particular a partnership between France and Germany as the foundation for a new Europe. Given the depth of wartime animosities, such an advocacy was courageous, but it should not be supposed that Churchill's consistent advocacy of 'United Europe', at home and abroad, indicated any belief that the United Kingdom could or should join in the enterprise of European reconciliation at an institutional level. His offer to France of 'Union' in 1940 was a gesture prompted by the gravity of the crisis, not the first expression of a continuing belief that Britain and France should formally unite. His relationship with de Gaulle during the war had always been difficult.[10] Sometimes he shared the American hostility to him, at others he accepted the need to see a restored France as part of the European balance and, with it, the assumed necessity of having to work with de

Gaulle in the post-war era. In the event, neither man was in power. In 1946–8 Churchill did not envisage a Franco-British relationship of special intimacy. It was for the Europeans to get on with building Europe. Britain, he supposed, would applaud and encourage – but only from the outside.

This analysis reflected his view, expressed with character-istic fulsomeness at a 'United Europe' rally in London in May 1947, that the 'World Temple of Peace' rested on four main pillars: the United States, the Soviet Union, the British Empire and Commonwealth, and Europe.[11] He did at the same time concede that Great Britain was 'profoundly blended' with 'Europe' but clearly not to the extent that its own separate 'pillar' status was jeopardised. At Fulton he spoke of 'the abiding power' of the British Empire and Commonwealth and painted a picture of '70 or 80 millions of Britons (as he called them) spread about the world, united in defence of their traditions.' The picture in fact looked a little different in Capetown, Canberra, Ottawa and Wellington but Churchill continued to suppose, as he always had done, that these detached Britons would respond 'as they always had done'.

The position of the British Empire was a little more complicated. In February 1947, after protracted but fruitless post-war negotiations, the Attlee government announced that British rule would end in the Indian sub-continent not later than June 1948. Given his well-known stance, Churchill could hardly do other than denounce 'the clattering down of the British Empire, with all its glories, and all the services it has rendered to mankind'. In the event, two new self-governing dominions of India and Pakistan arose in August 1947, amidst forecasts from Churchill (which sooner or later proved not inaccurate) of weak leadership, communal strife, loss of life and future disintegration. Yet, despite the strength of his language, he did not now suppose that he could prevent the 'loss' of India and confined himself to lugubrious prophecy and a certain pettiness towards Mountbatten for his role as the last Viceroy.[12]

These and other speeches reflect Churchill's preoccupation with power in the post-war world. The unpredictable fluidity of international relations always makes analysis difficult, and historians, no less than Churchill himself, are aware of the effect of the passage of time on their own assessments. Thus, as the Cold War became colder (and as subsequent volumes of *The Second World War* speedily appeared), Churchill's blunt assessment of Soviet imperialism appeared dazzlingly percep- tive. 'Revisionist' historians, in turn, found his stance provoc- ative. 'Post-revisionist' historiography reaches more balanced conclusions, while awaiting further evidence of Stalin's inten- tions from a Soviet state in internal crisis in the 1990s. The collapse of the '1945 system' in the Europe of today, and revelations of the nature of Stalinism, might in turn provide a vindication for Churchill's early and 'reactionary' denuncia- tion of 'Bolshevism'.

Churchill found his overseas excursions and statements rewarding. They provided confirmation that he possessed a kind of world-wide power. His speeches, whether at Fulton in 1946 or at The Hague in 1948, proved irritating and annoying to the Labour government, not so much because of what he said as because of the fact that he said it. To see Churchill feted by a President of the United States or by the 'European Movement', or to hear him described at the assembly of the new Council of Europe in 1949 as 'the first citizen of Europe' was not pleasing to the modest man who happened to be the King's first minister, Mr Attlee, or the immodest man, Mr Bevin, who served as Foreign Secretary. Labour MPs on the Left were even more irate at the extent to which it appeared that their government seemed in practice to follow a foreign policy which did not differ greatly in substance from what Churchill advocated. It is not altogether surprising, given his experience, but Churchill in this period was an exceptional Leader of the Opposition in the extent to which he shaped the national consensus. It was his view of the world which made the creation of a North Atlantic Treaty Organisation under a Labour government in 1949 seem vitally necessary.

Even so, the power which he exercised was not the power of a Prime Minister. He could not decide anything and his pronouncements on world affairs were not refreshed by the detailed information which only governments possess. The possibility that he might again exercise real power depended upon the overall performance in opposition of the Conserva- tive Party and the leadership which he gave it.

LEADER OF THE OPPOSITION 1945–1951

In opposition, Churchill was the celebrity virtuoso soloist who inspired by the brilliance of his individual performances (or alarmed by occasional wrong notes), rather than the leader of the orchestra who gave a constant and sustained lead to his fellow players. His temperament permitted no other course. He also conveniently believed that an opposition which sought to formulate for itself detailed policies was forfeiting the only pleasure which Opposition offered. At his age he was not open to alternative ways of behaving, though he sometimes went through the motions of discussion and consultation. Inevitably, there were accusations that he was 'out of touch' with the young men who came into the Commons for the first time in 1945 and found it very difficult to relate to their anxious concern to promote a new 'image' of Conservatism after the debacle of defeat. Their admiration for him remained, but it was a distant admiration without the dialogue on policy which they supposed would be a constant aspect of Opposition life.

Quite apart from the age-gap, the troubled history of his own relationship with the Conservative Party suggested a certain diffidence on party matters. *The Gathering Storm* waged retrospective warfare on Baldwin, Chamberlain and the kind of Conservative Party which they had led. Electorally, however, the Conservative Party of the 1930s had been conspicuously more successful than the Conservative Party under Churchill in 1945. Churchill chiefly directed his fire against their handling of foreign policy and he was now determined to keep the party in line in this respect. It was rather more difficult to say in general what Churchill thought 'Conservatism' was and how he believed the Conservative Party should develop. Although he had 'purged' leading Chamberlainites during the war, they had not entirely disappeared either from the party hierarchy or the backbenches. They were not altogether persuaded that they had behaved less responsibly than Churchill himself in the inter-war period or that Churchill's social and economic policies of the 1930s, where identifiable, offered shining guidance for the post-1945 world. The circumstances of his arrival at the leadership, coupled with egocentricity, age and literary preoccupation, meant that there were few intimate stalwart 'pillars' of the Conservative Party with whom Churchill was in constant contact and to whom he could turn for advice and comment. In any case, he had always preferred 'cronies' to 'pillars' and the supply of the former was beginning to run dry. He was disappointed by the defeat, amongst others, of Harold Macmillan, Duncan Sandys and his son Randolph in 1945. They hoped to get back to Westminster but until they did he lacked a useful and relatively youthful conduit which led him easily to the backbenches.

In addition, the question of the succession to his leadership could not be altogether avoided. Anthony Eden, his Foreign Secretary for most of the war, seemed to be the man.[13] Referring to him sometimes as his 'Princess Elizabeth' (that is to say the heir to his political 'throne'!), Churchill did formally leave Eden in charge during some of his absences abroad. The problem was that Eden's own particular expertise lay in the field of foreign policy (he had never held a domestic ministerial post) – just the area which Churchill continued so fluently to dominate. Eden was thus constantly in Churchill's shadow and was by no means brought fully into Winston's confidence before he made his pronouncements. It was a relationship of peculiar difficulty and importance. Churchill was not prepared to devolve to such an 'heir-apparent' the degree of power which might have passed to a specialist in domestic policy. There were times, too, when their close association over a decade inevitably produced differences of emphasis, from time to time, leading Churchill on occasion to wonder whether Eden after all was the man to succeed him. A less close overlap would have avoided the opportunity for such doubts. Eden in turn sometimes devoutly wished that the old man would go. After all, it was a decade or so ago that he and not Churchill had been seen as the 'coming man'.

The complexities of Conservatism in this period were further demonstrated by the appointment of R.A. Butler as chairman of the party's Research Department. As a loyal Chamberlainite Under-Secretary of State for Foreign Affairs during the years of the 'gathering storm', he had been lucky to escape banishment. He had gained in stature from piloting through the Commons the 1944 Education Act, and established in the process a reputation as an architect of the 'new Conservatism'. Churchill never liked him but felt obliged to offer him the Research Department in late 1945. In this position Butler encouraged young men to fashion new policies which it was hoped would make the party more attractive to the voters. Somewhat sceptical about these initiatives, Churchill did not involve himself in the detailed formulation of policy, though he still insisted on seeing the final versions and adding phrases of his own.

Butler took pride in the *Industrial Charter* of May 1947. Churchill did not veto its publication but neither did he display conspicuous enthusiasm for a rather bland document which accepted full employment as a goal and moved towards a 'mixed economy' insofar as it accepted the nationalisation of the Bank of England and the coal industry, though it opposed the future nationalisation of iron and steel. Churchill, flapping his arms slowly, attacked the 'gloomy state vultures of nationalisation' but the pre-1914 Liberal still lurking in him could see some circumstances in which nationalization might be beneficial, and the somewhat embattled Chancellor of 1925 had no great love for the independence of the Bank of England. By 1949, when *The Right Road* for Britain was ready, Churchill, as much by neglect as by design, had presided over the Conservative Party's potentially attractive reaction to the agenda set by Labour's 1945 victory. By 1949, too, according to Harold Nicolson, Churchill was working furiously at his war memoirs because he sensed that at the next election he would get back in and he wanted to finish the book before he became once again Prime Minister. He was now seventy five.

Political parties invariably explain their defeat, when all else fails, by referring to shortcomings in their organisation. That had been the case with the Conservatives in 1945, and in the following year Churchill had persuaded Lord Woolton, businessman and wartime Food Minister, to become Chairman of the party and to overhaul its administration. As in policy matters, however, he did so with a feeling, born of long experience, that it was governments which lost elections rather than Oppositions which won them. Organisational changes or new programmes would avail little until governments began to lose their way, either through their own blunders or circumstances beyond their control. A defence of his relaxed leadership in the early years after 1945 could rest in that argument. By 1949, however, Churchill sensed that his former Labour colleagues were tiring and that the Conservatives had a chance. What might be his final chance made him at once more imperious, impetuous and impatient – not least in his dealings with his children, some of whom shared these dispositions to the full and who could thus participate uninhibitedly in family rows, particularly when they emulated their father's consumption of alcohol but did not possess his self-control. There was room for reflection, not least by his wife, on the domestic price of the pursuit of power.

Polling – under Labour's 1948 Representation of the People Act – took place in February 1950. The outcome was tantalising. If Labour had retained anything like its 1945 majority and with it the prospect of another full administration there can be little doubt that Churchill would have had to resign the party leadership, either immediately or a little while into the life of the new government. In fact, Labour's majority was drastically reduced to a mere six, the most common explanation being that middle class voters, amongst whom were many Liberals, had returned to the Conservatives. It seemed most unlikely that Labour could survive anything like a full term. Churchill wanted to deliver the knock-out blow himself and, in the light of the result which he had achieved, there was little incentive to try to remove him. Indeed, the prospect of power reinvigorated him to an extraordinary degree. The further stroke which he had suffered in 1949 seemingly had not weakened him permanently. He husbanded his energy, was at pains to visit Marrakesh, and was keen to be seen in public watching his racehorses in action – a comparatively new enthusiasm.

Politically, he let loose an astonishing sequence of parliamentary speeches and procedural manoeuvres which contributed substantially to undermining Labour morale, already weakened by the illness of leading ministers, divisions relating to the Health Service, and the additional burdens arising out of the Korean War which began in June 1950. Although he was also working on the fifth volume of his war memoirs, *Closing the Ring*, which was to end on the eve of D-Day with the Hitler tyranny doomed, he could hardly wait for what might well be his last general election – whichever way it went. He had never liked Herbert Morrison, Bevin's successor as Labour Foreign Secretary, and their parliamentary exchanges were particularly barbed on Middle Eastern and other issues. At this point, Attlee, with his small majority, decided to seek a fresh mandate from the electorate.

It was against this background that in the October 1951 campaign Labour attempted to brand Churchill as a 'warmonger' and to suggest that only a Labour government stood in the way of a Third World War. The *Daily Mirror* asked its readers to consider whether it was Churchill's or Attlee's finger they wanted to see on the trigger. The Conservatives had hoped that they might be able to carry the election with their ambitious commitment to build 300,000 houses a year, but found, yet again, that it was on the person of Winston Churchill that attention centred. Apart from some withering remarks at Attlee's expense, however, he showed unexpected restraint. He replied to the charges by saying that he did not want any fingers upon any trigger. He did not believe a Third World War was inevitable but if one should occur it would not be a British finger that would pull the trigger.

The outcome of the election was very close but the Conservatives scraped home with a majority that was only slightly bigger than Labour's in the previous year. It would, however, provide Winston Churchill with a sufficient base for his last exercise of political power.

. . .

THE POPULAR PRIME MINISTER: OCTOBER 1951–APRIL 1955

Churchill, at long last, at the age of nearly seventy seven, won his first General Election.[14] His power rested at length on the people's choice, at least insofar as the electoral system had circumvented the fact that Labour received the largest total poll of all three parties. He celebrated his first popular endorsement by forming, in dribs and drabs, a Cabinet with the highest proportion of peers for thirty years, a selection which naturally irked aspiring Conservative MPs. His somewhat cavalier approach to forming a government stemmed in part from ignorance of the potential talent available to him and in part from his desire to have round about him men from former times whom he liked and trusted, no matter whether or not they had directly relevant political experience.

He liked the idea of coordinating ministers, quickly christened 'Overlords' in another wartime echo.[15] In came Lord Cherwell (Lindemann) as Paymaster-General, Lord Ismay as Commonwealth Secretary, Walter Monckton as Minister of Labour and Field-Marshal Lord Alexander of Tunis as Minister of Defence (as soon as he had completed his term as Governor-General of Canada). Meanwhile, Churchill thought he could do that job again himself. Eden was Foreign Secretary, Butler Chancellor of the Exchequer and Macmillan Minister of Housing. Churchill would have liked to include the leader of the Liberal Party, but he declined. This selection made it apparent that Churchill still saw himself as a national rather than a party leader.

Return to power seems to have given him initially fresh energy and enthusiasm. He still retained an interest in what his ministers were doing, though he no longer had quite the energy to inflict questions and suggestions on them at all hours of the day and night. Increasingly, he drew satisfaction from the fact of his survival rather than from the achievement of any specific short-term domestic ambitions. The immediate problems confronting the government remained basically economic, and the Prime Minister had few fresh ideas of his own to offer. He certainly did not suggest that his government should embark on a fundamental reconsideration of the National Health Service or 'privatise' (with the exception of steel) those industries which had been nationalised under Labour. Walter Monckton, as Minister of Labour, was to be conciliatory to the trade union movement. There was no need to restore the 1927 Trade Disputes Act which Labour had repealed. Macmillan was encouraged to produce the houses that had been promised. This emphasis almost appears to suggest that Churchill was doing his best to erase his reputation as a man of confrontation. It was also the case that to be conciliatory required less effort.

The effort he wanted still to make lay once again in the international field and he lost no time in seeking to relive the past. Only a few weeks after taking office, he embarked on the *Queen Mary* for the United States bent, yet again, on establishing a personal relationship with President Truman, in what was an election year. The State Department warned the President that he would be treated to a global survey in the grand manner but Churchill's real objective was 'To

buttress Britain's waning prestige and influence by demon-
strating a special relationship between the UK and the US.'
State Department officials urged that Truman should concur
in the importance of the relationship with Britain but should
stress that it proved most effective when it underlay other
multilateral relationships, such as NATO.

Churchill had been rumbled. There was still much personal
warmth towards him, but he would not receive the special
treatment he desired. Congress, in saluting his speech, was
acknowledging a voice from an earlier age but was not
inclined to give him the equipment he requested. Dean
Acheson, Truman's Secretary of State, thought that
Churchill's comments in conversation suffered from the
absence of familiarity with frustrating detail which the daily
pain of decision and action required. Churchill did not give
up hope, but nonetheless in his hotel bedroom he grieved,
according to his doctor, that England in her fallen state could
no longer address America as an equal but had to come cap
in hand to do Washington's bidding. One of the pillars of the
Temple of World Peace was evidently still strong, despite the
inconclusive outcome of the Korean War, but it was now very
conspicuously free-standing.[16]

The European pillar had strengthened since 1947 but by
the time Churchill returned to power it no longer required his
patronising benevolence. The European Coal and Steel Community had been negotiated in 1950 but the Labour government had declined to join. In the Commons in June Churchill
declared that 'national sovereignty is not inviolable'. It could
be resolutely diminished if such a step had common benefits.
Once back in power, however, he did not try to swing Britain
energetically into line with those Western European political
and economic trends of which the ECSC was the first
manifestation. He was suspicious of French proposals for a
European Defence Community.

Some mystery still attaches to Churchill's attitude at this
juncture. It certainly caused disappointment, made even more
acute because of his supposed former enthusiasm. It was the
case that Eden's bones were telling him that Britain could not
enter any kind of European Federation but, contrary to what
has sometimes been suggested, the Prime Minister was not
overborne by him. A different lead from the Prime Minister
might have encouraged other ministers who at least sub-

sequently claimed European enthusiasms. It may be that Churchill had a certain vision but lacked the drive to undertake its realisation. There was a limit, in any case, beyond which the British electorate would not at this juncture go, under any leader.[17]

It may be that for the moment Churchill was more exercised by the devastating significance of atomic weapons. Despite the cut-off of American information, the Labour government had proceeded with the development of a British atomic bomb. The first test took place in October 1952. Along with the United States and the Soviet Union, Britain now possessed a weapon which gave its possessor a unique kind of power. When the 'V-bombers' were ready to deliver, conventional forces could be reduced. As the first British Prime Minister to have such a weapon, Churchill was very conscious of the onerous additional responsibility that was his. He felt that its possession gave the British 'pillar' new strength but at the same time laid upon him, near the end of his life, the duty to make one last effort to reduce East-West tension. It would be the climax of his career.

International developments seemed to give him an opportunity. Even though he did not take to John Foster Dulles, the new Secretary of State, he hoped that wartime links with the new President, Eisenhower, would serve him in good stead. Little did he know that Eisenhower was writing in his diary in January 1953 that Churchill was 'quite definitely showing the effects of the passing years'. He was as charming and interesting as ever but in seeking to stress the special relationship he was trying to relive the days of World War II. 'Even if this picture were an accurate one of those days', he concluded, 'it would have no application to the present.'[18] The death of Stalin in March 1953 and the imminent end of the Korean War in 1953 encouraged Churchill to think that a 'Big Three' summit and some kind of new 'Locarno Treaty' might be possible. He told anyone who would listen that he still had this big task ahead of him. It was the supreme justification for remaining in office.

Churchill's stroke in the summer of 1953 caused the postponement of a preliminary meeting with Eisenhower. It was held in Bermuda in December, but the Americans were not to be persuaded of the merits of an early summit with the Soviet Union. However, through 1954 there were signs of some improvement in East-West relations, though much of the hard work fell on Eden in Berlin and Geneva. Churchill paid a further visit to Eisenhower in June 1954 and, on finding him still opposed to a summit with Malenkov, suggested that he should go to the Soviet Union on a 'reconnoitring patrol'. Such was Churchill's determination that it seems that he only informed his Cabinet colleagues of his plan after he had proposed a visit to Molotov. In the event, however, Churchill did not receive an invitation. Malenkov's fall in February 1955 and the subsequent need for the Bulganin–Khruschev regime to establish itself meant that Churchill's last opportunity to end his career on a high note as 'world peacemaker' had passed. On 5 April 1955, he at last tendered his resignation.

There is a poignancy and sadness about the last years of a man of power. Some of the accounts of his poor state of health and failing business competence in his second government are overstated. The one substantial study of Churchill's 'Indian Summer' rightly dismisses the notion that he was 'ga-ga' in this final phase, though it in turn perhaps gives too favourable a verdict. There is indeed a pathetic quality about this venerable old man which excites both sympathy and irritation. It was that same mixture of feelings which prevented many of his latter-day colleagues from acting towards him with that ruthlessness in the interests of the State which he had himself displayed. Convinced that he still had something to contribute which no one else could offer, he would not give up power and they lacked the courage to force him out. The capacity to let go is rare in a man of power, particularly when, as with Churchill, he does not see life *sub specie aeternitatis*. The self-centredness which had been a necessary element in his pursuit of power did not desert him at the end. Even though Eden had now married his niece, Churchill saw no reason to speed up the succession. It may be that Eden did not in fact have the qualities necessary in a Prime Minister, but the strain of waiting for the moment did not improve his already delicate nerves. In any event, the long-delayed 'transfer of power' turned out to be a disaster.

It would be wrong, of course, to convey the impression that the administration as a whole was an unmitigated disaster, but the fact was that at the end it was an octogenarian who presented the image of Britain to the world. It was an old man, dressed in yet one more strange costume who, amidst the pomp and pageantry of a Coronation in 1953, was the indomitable embodiment of a once great empire now struggling, with great spirit and dignity, but in vain, against the ravages of time.

. . . .

NOTES AND REFERENCES

1. B. Pimlott, ed., *The Second World War Diary of Hugh Dalton 1940–45*, London, 1986, p. 865.
2. Churchill, in his role as one of the 'Big Three', was first comprehensively studied by Herbert Feis, *Churchill, Roosevelt, Stalin: The War They Waged and The Peace They Sought*, Princeton, 1957. It should be compared with the new picture presented in Robin Edmonds, *The Big Three: Churchill, Roosevelt and Stalin*, London, 1991.
3. John Barnes and David Nicholson, eds., *The Empire at Bay: The Leo Amery Diaries 1929–1945*, London, 1988, p. 1046.
4. Chuter Ede, for example, wrote on 23 July in his diary that apart from G.R. Strauss, he knew of no one else who foretold an absolute majority for Labour. K. Jeffereys, ed., *Labour and the Wartime Coalition: From the Diary of James Chuter Ede*, London, 1987, p.226.
5. K.O. Morgan, *Labour in Power, 1945–1951*, Oxford, 1984, pp. 43–4. Beaverbrook claimed that he had been endeavouring to return Churchill to office and not his party, but 'The unpopularity of the party proved too strong for the greatness of Churchill and the affection in which he is held by the people.' Martin Gilbert, *'Never Despair': Winston S. Churchill 1945–1965*, London, 1988, p. 113.
6. See chapter 9 'Conservatism in Eclipse' in P. Addison, *The Road to 1945*, London, 1977 edn., pp. 229–69.
7. These issues are discussed from varying standpoints by C. Barnett, *The Audit of War. The Illusion and Reality of Britain as a Great Nation*, London, 1986; H.L. Smith, ed., *War and Social Change: British Society in the Second World War*, Manchester, 1986; K. Jefferys, 'British Politics and Social Policy during the Second World War', *Historical Journal*, xxx (1987), pp. 123–44.
8. T.H. Anderson, *The United States, Great Britain, and the Cold*

War 1944–1947, Columbia, 1981, pp. 113ff.: Fraser Harbutt, *The Iron Curtain. Churchill, America and the Origins of the Cold War*, Oxford, 1986.

9. Robin Edmonds, *Setting the Mould: The United States and Britain 1945–1950*, Oxford, 1986; William Roger Louis and Hedley Bull, eds., *The 'Special Relationship': Anglo-American Relations since 1945*, Oxford, 1986.

10. François Kersaudy, *Churchill and de Gaulle*, London, 1981.

11. J.W. Young, *Britain, France and the Unity of Europe 1945–1951*, Leicester, 1984, pp. 108–11.

12. J.G. Darwin, *Britain and Decolonisation: The Retreat from Empire in the Post-War World*, London, 1988, pp. 40–4.

13. The wartime relationship is intelligently explored in Elisabeth Barker, *Churchill and Eden at War*, London, 1978. Robert Rhodes James discusses their early post-war relationship in *Anthony Eden*, London, 1986, pp. 315–20.

14. Anthony Seldon, *Churchill's Indian Summer: The Conservative Government, 1951–55*, London, 1981, is the fullest account of this administration. He has subsequently written a shorter appraisal – 'The Churchill Administration, 1951–1955' – in Peter Hennessey and Anthony Seldon, eds., *Ruling Performance: British Governments from Attlee to Thatcher*, Oxford, 1987, pp. 63–97. See also the general appraisal in K.O. Morgan, *The People's Peace: British History 1945–1989*, Oxford, 1990, and in K. Middlemas, *Power, Competition and the State: Volume i: Britain in Search of Balance, 1940–1961*, London, 1986.

15. The 'Overlord' idea, and Churchill's concept of Cabinet, are discussed in Peter Hennessey, *Cabinet*, Oxford, 1986, pp. 47–52.

16. I am indebted for these quotations and the surrounding commentary to Raymond A. Callahan, *Churchill: Retreat from Empire*, Tunbridge Wells, 1984, pp. 260–1.

17. For a discussion of the 'sad disillusionment', amounting 'almost to a betrayal', words used by Harold Macmillan concerning European policy in the second Churchill government, see Michael Charlton, *The Price of Victory*, London, 1983, p. 124ff.

18. Robert H. Ferrell, ed., *The Eisenhower Diaries*, New York, 1981, pp. 222–3.

Chapter 7

EPILOGUE:
TRIUMPH AND TRAGEDY

The sixth volume of *The Second World War* which Churchill insisted on writing, against the better judgment of his publishers, appeared in 1953 as *Triumph and Tragedy*. It described the final stages of the war, and its purpose, in considerable measure, was to establish his prescience ahead of that division of Europe with which, as Prime Minister, he had to deal. Always, in his mind, the past provided justification for the present. It was that same passion which prompted him after his retirement to return to the writing of the *History of the English-Speaking Peoples*, that grand project which had been so rudely interrupted by the Second World War.[1] No other twentieth-century statesman, with the possible exception of de Gaulle, has had such an obsession with history and both the desire and the ability to be actor and chronicler in its most recent unfolding.

The tale was one of triumph and tragedy – global, continental, national, personal – a tale full of sound and fury. The man at its centre could not himself dwell peacefully in those sunlit uplands which he glimpsed. Churchill eclipsed all his great contemporaries in the profusion of adjectives which his character and behaviour attracted: bumptious, boorish, ambitious, pugnacious, audacious, courageous, ruthless, reckless, egocentric, romantic, radical, reactionary, pampered, parasitical, philistine, infantile – all of these words, in some combination or other, were used to describe him at various stages in his career. They were all appropriate, in one context or another. It is not surprising that an early burn-out was predicted. It was transparent that he could not pace himself and would dissipate his phenomenal energy in wild schemes.

The brilliance of their initial conception would be vitiated by his failure to work out their detailed implications. He lived always in the shadow of his father's meteoric rise and fall. His political card was marked for failure, though there would be excitements and achievements along the way. Lloyd George, himself no stranger to the Juggernaut of ambition, was only one of many to pronounce Churchill's political obituary, in this case writing to Frances Stevenson soon after Gallipoli:

> It is the Nemesis of the man who fought for this war for years. When the war came he saw in it the chance for glory for himself and has accordingly entered on a risky campaign without caring a straw for the misery and hardship it would bring to thousands, in the hope that he would prove to be the outstanding man in this war.[2]

It was a harsh and incorrect verdict and, ironically, the Nemesis that was to overtake Lloyd George within a few years proved to be enduring whilst Churchill's was only temporary. Churchill had not 'fought for' the Great War for years and he was not indifferent to the hardship the Gallipoli campaign would bring. It was true, however, that ancestry and experience combined to give Churchill a perspective on power which was awkward for his Liberal Cabinet colleagues. He had seen bodies on the battlefield and had known what it was to fight. Liberal England did not disown empire but even 'Liberal Imperialists' like Grey, Haldane or Asquith could not quite reconcile themselves to the brute force which had made it possible and which, in the last analysis, sustained it. Churchill did not want war, but his reading of European history told him that it had determined and would still determine the fate of states. It was a 'great illusion' to think otherwise. The Great War, however harrowing, had been a necessary war. Victory had made possible the survival of the British Empire.

Churchill continued to believe until the end of his life that this was a 'good thing', but it was a conviction that increasingly separated him from articulate sections of British opinion. It seemed to him absurd to suppose that Imperialism should be a source of shame. The British record was remarkable. Of course it rested ultimately upon force but so did all government. What mattered was whether rulers, whether indigenous or foreign, exercised their power reasonably and responsibly. He believed that the British did. His oracular claims in this regard struck a diminishing chord. The public did not necessarily dissent from his conclusion but was unwilling to contemplate the costs of maintaining an empire against the wishes of substantial sections of its inhabitants. In these matters Churchill swam against the tide and was not able to reverse it. His political base was exiguous. His personality seemed anachronistic.

The Second World War rescued him from the significant but minor position in twentieth-century British politics which he would otherwise have occupied. He was indeed the horse for the course. He was not changed overnight into a different kind of man, but now what mattered was tenacity, resolution and resource. He was in his element. Of course, there were mistakes and misjudgments to be set beside the achievements and the triumphs but, for Britain, insofar as any one person can be said to have 'won the war', Churchill was the man. However, although he did not brood endlessly, Tolstoy-like, on the frailty of a man supposedly possessing supreme power, he was uncomfortably aware of the great forces which swirled around him during the war. 'Power', when viewed from the top, was a puzzling and endlessly shifting combination of military, technological, economic and psychological strength. He had fused together 'British Power' to perhaps its maximum possible extent to survive and then to participate in victory. Half a century later it seems a remarkable if flawed performance. It also belongs to a world which seems remote.

It is possible that if he had been returned as Prime Minister in 1945 Churchill might have been able to slow down or to divert some of the pressures that crowded in on Britain in the post-war world. Immediately, for example, he might have had a useful influence in the deal that was reached at the Potsdam conference – concluded after he had left office. His policy in India or Palestine might have been significantly different, initially at least. Yet it is unlikely that he could have done other than what he said he would never do – preside over the liquidation of the British Empire.[3] His attitude to the Suez Canal zone during his second government suggests that he would have shown 'realism' when it came to the point. When 'British' was dropped from the 'Commonwealth of Nations' in 1952 Churchill acquiesced, with regret. Even so, the demise of the British Empire was as much a melancholy retreat as that of the sea of faith. It was painful and it was a tragedy. His own loss of power intertwined with that of the nation.

He became conscious, during his second government, though reluctantly and not without attempts to recapture old glories, that Britain was in decline, or at least his conception of Britain's rightful place in the world was in decline. His own hero, John Churchill, had taken a dukedom, and so could Winston himself if he had been minded to accept. The fact that he did not accept was perhaps an indication that despite his romantic positioning of himself in history he also possessed a shrewd awareness that he would 'last' better in the history books of the future as Sir Winston Churchill than as Duke of Dover or London.[4] That place would be indelibly secured by his role in 1940 above all, even when all due allowance has been made for the myths which have grown up around it.[5] He had relished power all his life but was apparently never to receive it in full measure. The war changed everything. Those who had suspected that there lurked within him a yearning to be a dictator were proved wrong, but so also were those who supposed that even a free people could survive without the smack of firm government.[6] It was a position 'above parties' (despite his necessary party allegiances) almost without parallel in modern British political history. By the same token, his legacy has been diffuse and increasingly difficult for any group or party easily to identify with.[7] He was a 'sport' who could never be repeated. In 1955, at the moment of retirement, he could look back on half a century in which, despite the inescapable conflicts of politics, he had played no small part in expanding a national consensus, cemented, so he supposed, by a deep and self-sufficent sense of Englishness.[8] The degree of national unity achieved under Churchill, as Michael Howard puts it, somewhat bleakly,'has been steadily eroded; that glorious flood tide which swept us all up together in a single national effort has ebbed, leaving a desolate foreshore littered with evil-smelling detritus and decay'.[9]

He was too old a man, however, too full of memories, to strike out boldly and incisively in a new direction. He could vent his fury against the presentation portrait of him by Graham Sutherland (and his wife was to have it destroyed)

170

but as had happened before to Churchill, a painter can grasp the final powerlessness even of a man of power.[10] To the end, however, he searched for a vision of the future for, without it, the handling of power was pointless. The imperial destiny had been so integral to his being and his life story, however, that although he caught a glimpse of a new Europe, he could not bring himself to contemplate the reorientation of national identity which its creation would entail. He still yearned for a 'special relationship' of the English-speaking peoples which was not obtainable on the terms he desired.

Nothing any single elderly man could do would reverse the current of change. He could even see, occasionally, that the crumbling of the world in which he had grown up was not without some hopeful aspects. He had moved most of his life, mentally and often actually, among the great men of power. He had been cut off, and cut himself off, from the everyday life of ordinary people. It was puzzling, but a fact, that the demise of empire, which he believed would have such dire consequences for the British people, was accompanied by a steady rise in the 'standard of living'. It might even eventually be the case that through the tragedy of war would come the lasting triumph of peace. It would not be a smooth inexorable path of progress but, like his own experience of life, full of setbacks and paradoxes. The power of the hydrogen bomb which the erstwhile horsebacked Hussar authorised as Prime Minister might 'by a process of sublime irony have reached a stage in this story where safety will be the sturdy child of terror, and survival the twin brother of annihilation'.[11] To the end of the curious history of the human race power was paradoxical. That was something to be grateful to 'Providence' for.

· · ·

NOTES AND REFERENCES

1. Christopher Parker, *The English Historical Tradition since 1850*, Edinburgh, 1990, does not even mention Churchill as a significant figure in that tradition, but *The History of the English-Speaking Peoples* continues to sell steadily, whatever the opinion of 'professionals' about its merits.
2. A.J.P. Taylor, ed., *Lloyd George, A Diary by Frances Stevenson*, London, 1971, p. 50.

3. 'Our first object', Churchill wrote in November 1951 in response to a paper on United Europe, 'is the unity and consolidation of the British Commonwealth and what is left of the former British Empire.' A.N. Porter and A.J. Stockwell, eds., *British Imperial Policy and Decolonization 1938–64: Volume 2, 1951–64*, London, 1989, p. 8.
4. D. Cannadine, *The Decline and Fall of the British Aristocracy*, London, 1990, p. 680.
5. I. Berlin, *Mr Churchill in 1940*, London, n.d. The essay originally appeared in 1949.
6. In the fevered atmosphere of the Abdication Crisis, for example, when there was speculation that King Edward VIII might be contemplating forming an Executive Government headed by a Dictator, Ramsay MacDonald wrote 'A person like Churchill might well put his hand to that job'. P. Ziegler, *Edward VIII*, London, 1990, p. 302.
7. J.H. Grainger, *Patriotisms, Britain: 1900–1939*, London, 1986, p. 356, comments that Churchill, unlike de Gaulle, 'left behind no political structure, no heritable idea – only a distinctive style to be adopted at peril'. Only Mrs Thatcher, amongst his successors, has attempted to wear the mantle of 'Winston' – at peril.
8. Dennis Smith, 'Englishness and the Liberal inheritance after 1886', in Robert Colls and Philip Dodd, eds., *Englishness: Politics and Culture 1880–1920*, London, 1986, p. 275, notes that when Churchill called on his countrymen to 'fight on the beaches' he was echoing Baldwin's 1924 view that 'The Englishman is made for a time of crisis.'
9. 'Churchill and the Era of National Unity' in Michael Howard, *The Lessons of History*, Oxford, 1991, pp. 158–9.
10. Roger Berthoud, *Graham Sutherland: A Biography*, London, 1982, pp.183–200, 299–302.
11. Cannadine, *Churchill's Speeches*, Harmondsworth, 1990, p. 345.

FURTHER READING

Winston Churchill properly features in practically every book which deals with twentieth-century British political history. The span and centrality of his career ensures a steady stream of comment, favourable and unfavourable, in almost every memoir and political biography. It would need a major bibliography to list all the items of relevance to his life and times. What follows is merely a selection of items designed to provide further guidance but still stopping far short of an exhaustive listing.

This study would not have been possible without the existence of the major official life of Churchill begun by his son, Randolph, and continued with exemplary dedication and thoroughness by Martin Gilbert. The publication of the seventh and final volume in 1988 brought to a conclusion an enterprise begun in 1966. The successive volumes, together with the 'companion' volumes, present the student with a rich array of information, at once enthralling 'in his own words' and make possible the kind of critical evaluation which is attempted in this volume. Martin Gilbert has distilled the essence of his work into a single but still very large volume, *Winston S. Churchill*, London, 1991.

Students without either time or energy to read the thousands of pages of the official life have many alternatives. Second World War books – Philip Guedalla, *Mr Churchill: a portrait* London, 1941; Lewis Broad, *Mr Churchill*, London, 1941; Guy Eden, *Portrait of Churchill*, London, 1945 – are only superficial, but they reveal contemporary attitudes towards him. Charles Eade, ed., *Churchill by his contemporaries*, London, 1953, is likewise helpful. The essays in A.J.P. Taylor, ed.,

Churchill: Four Faces and the Man, London, 1969, concentrate on different facets of his personality and abilities. So do the contributions in Peter Stansky, ed., *Churchill: a profile*, London, 1973. Among the biographies, the following are particularly recommended: H.M. Pelling, *Winston Churchill*, London, 1974, new edn. 1990; Piers Brendon, *Winston Churchill: A Brief Life*, London, 1984; Ted Morgan, *Churchill 1974–1915*, London, 1983; the (second) Earl of Birkenhead, *Churchill 1874–1922*, London, 1990. William Manchester is engaged on a trilogy, two volumes of which have so far appeared: *The Last Lion: Winston Spencer Churchill: Visions of Glory 1874–1932*, London, 1983, and *The Caged Lion: Winston Spencer Churchill* London, 1988. Manchester presents a very 'Churchillian' view of Churchill.

Personal impressions, from various angles, appear in Violet Bonham-Carter, Baroness Asquith, *Winston Churchill as I knew him*, London, 1965; Charles Wilson, Lord Moran, *Winston Churchill: the struggle for survival, 1940–1965*, London, 1966; Sir John Wheeler-Bennett, ed., *Action This Day: Working with Churchill*, London, 1968; R.W. Thompson, *Churchill and Morton*, London, 1976; S.G. Pawle, *The War and Colonel Warden*, London, 1963; Sir John Colville, *The Churchillians*, London, 1981; Sir Evelyn Shuckburgh, *Descent to Suez: Diaries 1951–1956*, London, 1986; Sir John Colville, *The Fringes of Power: Downing Street Diaries 1939–1955*, London, 1985.

The best of the photographic books are R.S. Churchill and Helmut Gernsheim, comps., *Churchill: his life in photographs*, London, 1955, and M.J. Gilbert, *Churchill: a photographic portrait*, London, 1974.

Particular aspects of Churchill's career and character are covered by: Robert H. Pilpel, *Churchill in America, 1895–1961: an affectionate portrait*, London, 1976; Robert Rhodes James, *Churchill: A Study in Failure, 1900–1939*, London, 1970; M.J. Gilbert, *Winston Churchill: the wilderness years*, London, 1981; Brian Gardner, *Churchill in his Times: A Study in a Reputation, 1939–1945*, London, 1978; A. Seldon, *Churchill's Indian Summer: The Conservative Government, 1951–55*, London, 1981; J.D.B. Miller, *Sir Winston Churchill and the Commonwealth of nations*, St Lucia, Queensland, 1967; Raymond A. Callahan, *Churchill: Retreat from Empire*, Tunbridge Wells, 1984; M.C. Brommage, *Churchill and Ireland*, Notre Dame, 1964; M.J. Cohen, *Churchill and the Jews*, Oxford, 1986; Stuart Ball, *Baldwin and the*

Conservative Party: The Crisis of 1925–31, London, 1988; Neville Thompson, *The Anti-Appeasers: Conservative Opposition to Appeasement in the 1930s*, Oxford, 1971.

Churchill is evaluated as war leader in the following: Sir Isaiah Berlin, *Mr Churchill in 1940*, London, n.d., first published in 1949; J. Ehrman, 'Lloyd George and Churchill as war leaders', *Transactions of the Royal Historical Society*, vol. 11, 1961; J.M. Lee, *The Churchill Coalition 1940–1945*, London 1980; Patrick Cosgrave, *Churchill at War*, Vol. 1, *Alone 1939–1940*, London, 1974; David Jablonsky, *Churchill, The Great Game and Total War*, London, 1991; Michael Howard, 'Churchill and the Era of National Unity' in his *The Lessons of History*, Oxford, 1991; R. Lewin, *Churchill as Warlord*, London, 1973; A.J. Marder, *Churchill is Back: Churchill at the Admiralty, 1939–1940*, London, 1972; S.W. Roskill, *Churchill and the Admirals*, London, 1977; Sir Peter Gretton, *Former Naval Person: Winston Churchill and the Royal Navy*, London, 1968; Barrie Pitt, *Churchill and the Generals*, London, 1981; Sir Arthur Bryant, ed., *The Turn of the Tide*, London, 1957, and *Triumph in the West*, London, 1959 (the Alanbrooke Diaries).

Specific political relationships with individuals are treated in the following: R. Hyam, *Elgin and Churchill at the Colonial Office 1905–1908: The Watershed of the Empire-Commonwealth*, London, 1968; Kenneth Young, *Churchill and Beaverbrook*, London, 1966; David Day, *Menzies and Churchill at War*, London, 1986; E. Barker, *Churchill and Eden at War*, London, 1978; J.P. Lash, *Roosevelt and Churchill, 1939–41*, London, 1977; Warren F. Kimball, ed., *Churchill and Roosevelt: The Complete Correspondence*, Princeton, 1984; F. Kersaudy, *Churchill and de Gaulle*, London, 1981; H. Feis, *Churchill, Roosevelt, Stalin: The War They Waged and The Peace They Sought*, Princeton, 1957; R. Edmonds, *The Big Three: Churchill, Roosevelt and Stalin*, London, 1991.

Churchill's political ideas are discussed in M.J. Gilbert, *Churchill's Political Philosophy*, London, 1981; P. Addison, 'The Political Beliefs of Winston Churchill', *Transactions of the Royal Historical Society*, Fifth Series, vol. 30, 1980, and M. Cowling, *Religion and Public Doctrine in Modern England*, Cambridge, 1980. His own writings have been helpfully listed in Frederick Woods, *A Bibliography of the Works of Sir Winston Churchill*, rev. edn. 1975. The most prominent of his works have been listed in the chronology of this book. Robert Rhodes

James edited *The Complete Speeches of Sir Winston Churchill, 1897–1963*, New York, 1974. David Cannadine has made a useful recent selection, *Churchill's Speeches*, Harmondsworth, 1990. Churchill as historian is considered by M. Ashley, *Churchill as Historian*, London, 1968, and by J.H. Plumb in *The Making of an Historian: The Collected Essays of J.H. Plumb*, Volume i, London, 1988. One famous work is subjected to scrutiny by Robin Prior, *Churchill's 'World Crisis' as History*, London, 1983. Denis Bardens considers *Churchill in Parliament*, London, 1967. Kay Halle compiled *Impossible Churchill: a Treasury of Winston Churchill's Wit*, New York, 1966.

Sketches of Churchill and his political contemporaries appear in Keith Robbins, ed., *The Blackwell Biographical Dictionary of British Political Life in the Twentieth Century*, Oxford, 1990, and the fate of the Great Power, so closely intertwined with Churchill's own career, is considered in Keith Robbins, *The Eclipse of a Great Power: Modern Britain, 1870–1975*, London, 1983.

CHRONOLOGY AND PUBLICATIONS

1874 Born at Blenheim Palace, Oxfordshire, 30 November

1886 Lord Randolph Churchill, Chancellor of the Exchequer, August–December.

1888 Attends Harrow School

1893 Enters Sandhurst (Royal Military College)

1895 Death of Lord Randolph Churchill, 24 January
Commissioned and joins 4th Hussars
Visits Cuba, via United States, October–December

1896 Posted to India, October

1898 *The Story of the Malakand Field Force* published
Takes part in Battle of Omdurman, September

1899 Leaves India, March
The River War
To South Africa for the *Morning Post*, October
Captured by the Boers, November
Escapes, December

1900 *Savrola*
London to Ladysmith via Pretoria
Ian Hamilton's March
Elected Unionist MP for Oldham, October

1904 Joins Liberal Party, May

1905 Parliamentary Under-Secretary for the Colonies, December

1906 Elected Liberal MP for Manchester North West, January
Lord Randolph Churchill

1908 President of the Board of Trade, defeated as Liberal MP for Manchester North West and elected as Liberal MP for Dundee, April Marries Clementine Hozier, September
My African Journey

1909 *Liberalism and the Social Problem*

1910 Home Secretary, February
The People's Rights

1911 'Siege of Sidney Street', January
First Lord of the Admiralty, October

1914 At Antwerp, October

1915 Naval Attack on the Dardanelles, February
Coalition government, Chancellor of the Duchy of Lancaster, May Resigns office and goes to the Western Front, November

1916 Commands 6th Battalion, Royal Scots Fusiliers, January–May

1917 Minister of Munitions, July

1919 Secretary of State for War and Air, January

1921 Secretary of State for the Colonies (retaining Air Ministry until May 1921)

1922 Buys Chartwell Manor, Kent, September
Fall of Lloyd George Coalition. Defeated at Dundee, November

1923 First volume of *The World Crisis* (fifth and last volume 1931)
Fails to win West Leicester as Liberal, December

1924 Fails to win Abbey Division of Westminster as Independent Anti-Socialist, March
Elected for Epping as Constitutionalist, Chancellor of the Exchequer

1925 Returns Britain to the Gold Standard, April

1926 General Strike, May

1929 Defeat of Baldwin in General Election, elected for Epping, May

1930 *My Early Life*

1931 Resigns from Shadow Cabinet over India, January
India
Elected for Epping, October

1932 *Thoughts and Adventures*

1933 *Marlborough: His Life and Times* (fourth and last volume 1938)

1935 Joins Air Defence Research sub-committee

1936 Supports King Edward VIII During Abdication crisis, December

1937 *Great Contemporaries*

1938 *Arms and the Covenant*

1939 *Step by Step, 1936–1939*
First Lord of the Admiralty, September

1940 Prime Minister and Minister of Defence, 10 May

1941 British-Soviet agreement, July

1941 'Atlantic Charter', August
Declares war on Japan after Pearl Harbor. Addresses
Congress, December
Into Battle

1942 Fall of Singapore, governmental changes, February
To Cairo and Moscow, August
Victory at El Alamein, November

1943 Casablanca conference agrees on 'unconditional sur-
render', January
To Washington and Algiers, May
First Quebec conference, August
Teheran conference, November
Illness in North Africa, December

1944 D-Day landing, June
Second Quebec Conference, September
Conference with Stalin, Moscow, October
In Athens, December

1945 Yalta Conference, February
VE Day, 8 May
'Caretaker government' formed, 23 May
Potsdam Conference, July
Elected National Conservative MP for Woodford but
Labour wins General Election, 26 July

1946 'Iron Curtain' speech, Fulton, Missouri

1948 *The Second World War* (last volume published 1954)
Attends The Hague 'United Europe' conference
The Sinews of Peace

1949 Attends first session of Council of Europe at Strasbourg

1950 Labour wins General Election, Conservative MP for Woodford, February
Europe Unite

1951 Conservatives win General Election, Prime Minister, October, and Minister of Defence (until March 1952)
In the Balance

1952 *The War Speeches*

1953 Awarded Nobel Prize for Literature, October
Stemming the Tide

1955 Resigns as Prime Minister, 5 April

1956 *A History of the English-Speaking Peoples* (last volume 1958)

1961 *The Unwritten Alliance*

1964 Leaves House of Commons

1965 Dies in London, 24 January
State Funeral, 30 January. Buried in Bladon churchyard, near Blenheim, Oxfordshire

INDEX

INDEX

Tito, J.B., 141
Tobruk, 136
Tonypandy, 47
Tory Democracy, 7, 19
Truman, H.S., 146, 155–6, 162

Ulster, 8, 55–7
United States, 14, 30–1, 79, 111, 132–6, 152–3

Vanderbilt, Consuelo, 3
Victoria, Queen, 8, 31

Wales, Prince of (Edward VII), 5, 22, 33, 44
Wavell, Sir Archibald (Lord), 130
Wilson, Sir Arthur, 52
Wood, Sir Kingsley, 123
Woodstock, 2, 4–5
Woolton, Lord, 158

Yalta conference, 140